FINDING GOD IN THE
GARDEN

FINDING GOD IN THE
GARDEN

Planting, Pruning, and the Plan of Happiness

BRENT & WENDY TOP

DESERET
BOOK

Salt Lake City, Utah

Library of Congress Cataloging-in-Publication Data
Top, Brent L.
   Finding God in the garden : planting, pruning, and the plan of happiness / Brent L. Top and Wendy C. Top.
     p. cm.
  Includes bibliographical references.
  ISBN 978-1-60641-230-5 (paperbound)
   1. Spiritual life—The Church of Jesus Christ of Latter-day Saints.   2. Gardening—Religious aspects.   3. Gardens—Religious aspects.   I. Top, Wendy C.   II. Title.
  BX8656.T64 2010
  248.4'893—dc22   2009046672

Printed in the United States of America
Inland Graphics, Menomonee Falls, WI

10 9 8 7 6 5 4 3 2 1

CONTENTS

All things are created and made to bear record of me,
both things which are temporal, and things which are spiritual.

MOSES 6:63

PREFACE

We love to garden. Now, don't assume that we are very good at it, because we are not. We have never been selected as Yard of the Week by our community. No one stops by and asks to see our garden. We have never been invited to be part of the many home and garden tours. There has been no photo spread in *Better Homes and Gardens*. Nor will anyone confuse our yard with the gardens at Temple Square or our vegetable garden with the Victory Garden from public television. If you do see our yard on television, it will only be because someone submitted our name to be featured on a yard and garden episode of *Extreme Makeover*. We feel lucky if we can keep the grass green, the flowers in bloom, worms out of the fruit, and harvest an ear of sweet corn or a juicy, fresh tomato before the snow flies. We certainly are not experts when it comes to gardening, but we love it nonetheless. We haven't always felt that way, however.

Our parents loved to garden. They had beautiful yards, flower beds, and vegetable gardens. When we were young, we didn't appreciate gardening, let alone love it. That was probably because we viewed gardening as work, and as kids we preferred games to chores. We certainly enjoyed the fruits of our parents' gardens—freshly cut roses, corn on the cob, new potatoes, and most of all, raspberries. In our youth, the fruits and vegetables seemed sweeter and the flowers more beautiful if someone else did the work of weeding and watering and pruning and picking. As we have grown older, perhaps we have also grown wiser. Now we love gardening, not just partaking of the fruits of the garden. We can see more clearly now that the fruits of our garden are much sweeter and more enjoyable *because* we had to work so hard.

Shortly after we were married, we moved into a typical newlywed student apartment. A small plot, about six feet by six feet, near the apartment building had nothing but weeds growing in it. The landlord gave us permission to whack down the weeds, prepare the soil, and plant a garden, as long as we paid for the water and didn't ask for help. It wasn't like we really *wanted* a garden—we didn't need any extra work at the time. We had a different motivation, something that changed our view of gardening forever.

Spencer W. Kimball was president of the Church at that time, and we had heard him counsel the Saints to grow gardens and beautify their property. This was a theme he reiterated many times and in many settings:

"Grow all the food that you possibly can on your own property, if water is available; berry bushes, grapevines, and fruit trees are most desirable. Plant them if your climate is right for their growth. Grow vegetables and eat those grown in your own yard. Even those residing in apartments or condominiums can generally grow a little food in pots and planters" ("True Way of Life and Salvation," 4).

"Should evil times come, many might wish they had filled all their fruit bottles and cultivated a garden in their backyards and planted a few fruit trees and berry bushes and provided for their own commodity needs" ("God Will Not Be Mocked," 4).

"We are highly pleased with the response to the planting of gardens. It is health building, both from the raising of crops and the eating of them. It is delightful to see so many gardens all over the land, and reports come in from numerous families and individuals who have obtained much saving and pleasure in the planting of gardens. We hope this will be a permanent experience of our people, that they will raise much of what they use on their table" ("Foundations of Righteousness," 4).

We had no delusions of garden grandeur—of providing all of our needs from our small student apartment garden plot, saving tons of money, or recreating a Garden of Eden–like paradisiacal existence. We got into gardening in those early married years simply because we desired to follow the counsel of the living prophet. That first little garden, planted and

cared for as an act of obedience, gave us an introductory glimpse into the blessings that can be obtained and the lessons that can be learned in the garden. We probably spent a lot more money than we saved by having that garden, but we discovered then and have rediscovered with every growing season since that the spiritual blessings outweigh the temporal returns. "Even if the tomato you eat is a $2.00 tomato," President Kimball taught, "it will bring satisfaction anyway and remind us all of the law of the harvest, which is relentless in life. We do reap what we sow. Even if the plot of soil you cultivate, plant, and harvest is a small one, it brings human nature closer to nature as was the case in the beginning with our first parents" ("Listen to the Prophets," 76).

In the many years and gardens since that first attempt, we have learned many things. We have taken horticulture classes and listened faithfully to weekly gardening shows on the radio. We have read books, talked with experts, and visited world-class gardens in many places. We have learned by trial and error. Yet we are not experts by any means. Well, then, why in the world would we write a book about gardening? Perhaps the answer is that this book is not as much about gardening as it is about coming to know God and His gospel. It isn't as much about the lessons we have learned about peas, petunias, or perennials as it is about principles and people. We have learned much about shrubs and succulents but have learned far more about ourselves. We have partaken of the fruits of our own labors, but more important, we have tasted of the fruits of the gospel and gained a greater appreciation for the handiwork of God and His works in our own lives.

Alma taught that "all things denote there is a God; yea, even the earth, and all things that are upon the face of it" (Alma 30:44). Truly, all things are the typifying of Christ.

We see Him, His love, His mercy, His goodness all around us, even (or perhaps especially) in the garden as we till the soil, plant the seeds and start the new plants, and weed and prune and pick until our backs ache and our hands are dry and chapped. That is why we wrote this book—to share with you some of the lessons we have learned and insights we have gained in the garden, lessons that have changed our lives. We can't guarantee that your garden will dramatically improve by your reading this book. We hope, however, that *you* will improve—that your view of God and His "great plan of happiness" will expand (Alma 42:8), that your understanding of the principles of His gospel will increase, and that your desires to serve the Lord and your fellowmen will be magnified. These are a few of the small seeds of faith that have sprouted and are growing vigorously in our souls, seeds that grow into large spiritual trees of life that bear fruit that is "desirable to make one happy" (1 Nephi 8:10).

We have experienced for ourselves, both in gardening and in gaining testimonies, the pure truth of the words of Alma as he taught about experimenting upon the word of God by planting it within our humbled hearts as if it were a seed sown in softened soil. Our experiences both temporally and spiritually parallel the horticultural metaphors alluded to by Alma:

"Now, we will compare the word unto a seed. Now, if ye give place, that a seed may be planted in your heart, behold, if it be a true seed, or a good seed, if ye do not cast it out by your unbelief, that ye will resist the Spirit of the Lord, behold, it will begin to swell within your breasts; and when you feel these swelling motions, ye will begin to say within yourselves—It must needs be that this is a good seed, or that the word is good, for it beginneth to enlarge my soul; yea, it beginneth to enlighten my understanding, yea, it beginneth to be delicious to me. . . .

"And behold, as the tree beginneth to grow, ye will say: Let us nourish it with great care, that it may get root, that it may grow up, and bring forth fruit unto us. And now behold, if ye nourish it with much care it will get root, and grow up, and bring forth fruit.

"But if ye neglect the tree, and take no thought for its nourishment, behold it will not get any root; and when the heat of the sun cometh and scorcheth it, because it hath no root it withers away, and ye pluck it up and cast it out. . . .

"And thus, if ye will not nourish the word, looking forward with an eye of faith to the fruit thereof, ye can never pluck of the fruit of the tree of life.

"But if ye will nourish the word, yea, nourish the tree as it beginneth to grow, by your faith with great diligence, and with patience, looking forward to the fruit thereof, it shall take root; and behold it shall be a tree springing up unto everlasting life.

"And because of your diligence and your faith and your patience with the word in

nourishing it, that it may take root in you, behold, by and by ye shall pluck the fruit thereof, which is most precious, which is sweet above all that is sweet, and which is white above all that is white, yea, and pure above all that is pure; and ye shall feast upon this fruit even until ye are filled, that ye hunger not, neither shall ye thirst.

"Then, my brethren, ye shall reap the rewards of your faith, and your diligence, and patience, and long-suffering, waiting for the tree to bring forth fruit unto you" (Alma 32:28–43).

We have reflected again and again upon this allegory through the years as we have learned the lessons of gardening and of the gospel. Without fail, the principles of gardening verify or bear witness of the principles of life and eternal truth. We have organized the sections of this book to more or less follow the process laid out in this allegory and also to reflect the circle of life—birth, life, death, rebirth; sowing, cultivating, reaping. This small book does not contain all the things we have learned or that could be learned from gardening. An entire library could not do that. Our objective, however, is to share a few of our own experiences and insights in an effort to stimulate your own thinking, inspire you to see the lessons of life and the symbols of Christ and His love that are all around you, and help you cultivate your own seeds of faith.

SPRING-CLEANING

As soon as the snow melts and the sure signs of spring begin to appear, we are out in the yard and the garden. It feels so good to once again work the soil and do yard work. As excited as we always are when spring arrives, we are quickly reminded that good gardens require work—a lot of it. Gone are the days of Eden when flowers bloomed and trees and vines bore fruit spontaneously. All you have to do is look at your yard and garden in early spring to recognize that! Remnants of winter can be seen all around. There are those pesky leaves that fell after the last autumn raking or blew into corners and crevices with the icy winds. In the flower beds are dead plants—summer annuals and the foliage of perennials killed by old Jack Frost—that have to be removed. Unfortunately, winter almost always kills some branches in trees and bushes. Good gardeners know that summer growth, no matter how vigorous and vibrant, can't totally cover up unsightly dead branches and decomposing leaves. As a result, you see the gardeners at Temple Square and grounds crews at other impressive gardens clearing out the old to make ready for the new. Without spring-cleaning, summer gardens fall short of their glorious potential. So it is with people.

The term *spring-cleaning* is probably more often associated with the cleaning of houses than with cleaning yards and gardens. During the Victorian era, most homes were heated with wood-burning fireplaces and/or coal-burning stoves and were often lighted by oil-burning lamps. These produced soot, which accumulated in the houses on shelves, on window sills, on furniture, and even in bedding. No doubt cold-air inversions in mountain valleys trapped even more of the unsightly and unhealthy residue during the winter months. As the weather warmed, houses were cleaned from top to bottom of the winter accumulation of soot. The annual ritual became known as spring-cleaning.

When our family lived in Israel several years ago, we gained a greater appreciation for the notion of spring-cleaning as it relates to people. A Jewish holy day that occurs each spring is *Pesach*. We know it as Passover (most of us are somewhat familiar with it from reading the Old Testament). Immediately before this most significant celebration, devout Jews thoroughly clean their homes and places of business. The reason for this is that Passover is also called the "feast of unleavened bread" (Exodus 12:17), and products containing yeast or leavening of any kind are forbidden during this week-long commemoration. Grocery stores remove it from their shelves or cover it so it cannot be sold to anyone, including Gentiles. Restaurants serve sandwiches or pizza made with flat, unleavened crackers known as *matzot*. It is fascinating to observe. Private residences are also thoroughly cleaned. Every nook and cranny is swept bare from top to bottom so that no yeast or crumb of bread or anything remotely related to leavening can be found. To observant Jews at Passover, leavening represents death, decay, corruption, and uncleanness. This spring-cleaning is a very literal act that symbolically represents the need to continually cleanse from our lives any remnant of spiritual decay.

Each of us has both formal and informal ways whereby we can experience a spiritual spring-cleaning. On Sundays we have an opportunity to carefully examine ourselves, looking for anything and everything that stifles spiritual growth and shades us from life-giving Light. With the sacred sacramental covenant we promise, through the power of the Atonement of our Savior, to clean out the corruption and decay of our lives, whether big and unsightly or small and hidden from view. In a less formal way but just as spiritually significant, we can experience a spring-cleaning as we daily kneel before our Maker in personal and family prayers and as we pray unceasingly in our hearts throughout the day. There we may humbly and continually confess our sins and weaknesses, ask for forgiveness, and recommit ourselves to nourishing our faith by turning *from* sin and turning *to* God with increased love and devotion. This kind of spiritual cleaning doesn't have to be just in springtime. In fact, it must not be. It needs to be persistent and perpetual. Repenting and improving each day through the grace and mercy of Christ makes us more

pure and spiritually beautiful to the Master Gardener and more capable of bearing the kinds of blooms and fruits that glorify Him.

Not long ago, we hosted a ward party in our backyard. In preparation, we carefully weeded the flower beds, mowed and trimmed the grass, and discarded all the unsightly things we had cleaned out of the garden. We weren't trying to impress anybody but wanted it to be nice and pleasing for all who would be there. In a way, it was our offering to the ward—our contribution to the success of the party, a contribution that was offered in love for our friends.

Our lives are like a garden to be presented to the King of Kings as a gift of love and ultimate tribute. As the Book of Mormon admonishes, "Offer your whole souls as an offering unto him" (Omni 1:26). It goes without saying that we would want that garden to be cleaned and cleared of anything and everything that is unsightly or displeasing to the King. That requires spring cleaning, summer cleaning, fall cleaning, winter cleaning—in short, continual cleaning. Then we can feel confident that our offering is acceptable. As we clear out the winterkill from our garden and flower beds each spring, plowing them under and preparing the soil, we are reminded that every day we are cleaning and cultivating the garden of our souls that we may humbly present ourselves to the Master Gardener, prepared for the seeds of faith He desires to sow within us.

THE WARMTH OF THE SUN

Preparation precedes productivity in the garden. Flower beds must be prepared. Soil must be amended with organic material. Likewise, the vegetable garden must be tilled. The smell of soil is invigorating, and dirt under the fingernails is attractive, at least for a little while. Shopping trips to the nursery to pick out bedding plants and seeds are as exciting to us as a trip to Disneyland is for our grandchildren. The vegetable seeds are planted carefully in rows, straight as an arrow and evenly spaced. Beautiful annuals are carefully planted in the flower beds, and tomato and pepper plants are transplanted in the gardens. While we wait for the seeds to sprout, the bedding plants attract most of our attention. It is an exciting time. By the same token, it can be a frustrating time. Some years it seems as if it takes forever for the seeds to sprout and pop their heads up out of the ground. Sometimes the bedding plants don't seem to be doing anything—no new growth, no new leaves or buds, nothing. Sometimes they don't do well at all. It is discouraging. What in the world have we done wrong? We carefully prepared the soil. The sun is shining brightly. But the plants still aren't thriving. We selected the best seeds possible and the most vigorous bedding plants we could. We should know better, but it seems as if we have to learn this lesson all over again every spring: some things are out of our control.

We have learned that it doesn't matter that you have the best seeds and plants, a carefully prepared garden, and lots of light and water if you don't also have the warmth of the sun! Seeds won't germinate and plants won't grow until the soil is warm enough. Ground temperature is critical to productivity.

It has been our experience that people are like plants in this way. We all do better in the warmth of an environment filled with love and affection, kindness and consideration, appreciation and respect. Seeds of faith, sown by gospel instruction both at church and at home, will not produce the fruit we desire if the temperature, or emotional warmth, is insufficient. Faith is fortified by love. Testimony is nurtured with affection. Spirituality is cultivated in a warm environment of emotional closeness. In contrast, cold spells and killing frosts cause more damage to the emotional and spiritual growth of people than their physical counterparts do to plants. Plants can be replaced; people can't. The old adage certainly applies: "I don't care how much you know until I know how much you care." The Prophet Joseph Smith said it best: "Nothing is so much calculated to lead people to forsake sin as to take them by the hand, and watch over them with tenderness. When persons manifest the least kindness and love to me, O what power it has over my mind, while the opposite course has a tendency to harrow up all the harsh feelings and depress the human mind" (*History of the Church,* 5:23–24).

Perhaps this principle is manifest most profoundly in the home. As parents, we are gardeners, continually planting seeds of faith as we teach and nurture our children. The seeds are the teachings of the gospel of Jesus Christ and principles of civility, responsibility, and morality. We know the seeds are good, but no matter how carefully we plant them, they will not sprout and take root without warmth. Daily doses of affection—hugs and such expressions as "I love you," "Thank you," and "You mean so much to me"—are like rays of sunshine that continually contribute to the warm temperature of the heart. Love is the greatest root starter.

For each of us, the ultimate source of warmth is the Savior Himself, He who is "in the sun, and the light of the sun . . . —the light which is in all things, which giveth life to all things" (D&C 88:7–13). Plants need the warmth of the sun and so do we. We can't live without it. But what we need most and what enables us to bear fruit is the warmth of the Son. The more we feel that warmth in our personal lives, the more we will grow spiritually, the deeper the roots of our conversion will be, and the more productive our service to God and our fellowmen will be. The warmth of the Son is the pure love of Christ, which "never faileth. . . . and it endureth forever; and whoso is found possessed of it at the last day, it shall be well with him" (Moroni 7:46–47).

THE ETERNAL PROCESS OF CREATION

How often do we stop in the springtime to marvel at the emergence of delicately formed buds and blossoms that erupt from seemingly lifeless, barren trees or to wonder at green sprouts that materialize out of plain dirt and quickly differentiate into an infinite variety of plants? Do we realize we are watching the miraculous eternal process of creation? Do we take for granted the power of the warming sun as it harnesses and organizes the elements of the soil, air, and water into remarkably beautiful, complex, and godly creations that mortals can never hope to come close to replicating? "Even Solomon in all his glory was not arrayed like one of these," observed the Creator Himself of the lilies of the field (Matthew 6:29). Man's most exacting scientific investigation may hope to explain the mechanics of it but can never approach the wondrous creative life force that drives it. Not only does each growing substance have the light of life within it but even the tiniest division of it seems to know exactly what it must do to help create the intricate wondrous whole.

As children of the Creator, we have the blueprint for this endless creativity within us also. Godliness cannot exist without creating something good; indeed, God is the source and essence of all goodness and creativity. The urge or need to create something that will bless a life is righteous and godly. President Brigham Young taught that "the difference between God and the Devil is that God creates and organizes, while the whole study of the Devil is to destroy." Neither of them can do otherwise, for it is not in their nature. This means Satan and those who do his will are the only beings who really have no creativity. "Show me one principle that has originated [been created] by the power of the Devil. You cannot do it. I call evil inverted good, or a correct principle made an evil use of," said President Young. "But that which is of God is pure, lovely, holy and full of all excellency and truth, no matter where it is found, in hell, in heaven, upon the earth, or in the planets" (*Discourses of Brigham Young*, 69).

Thus, whenever we choose to do good, we create. This is an eternal principle.

Further, President Dieter F. Uchtdorf, second counselor in the First Presidency, affirmed that all of God's children are born to create:

"The desire to create is one of the deepest yearnings of the human soul. No matter our talents, education, backgrounds, or abilities, we each have an inherent wish to create something that did not exist before.

"Everyone can create. You don't need money, position, or influence in order to create something of substance or beauty.

"Creation brings deep satisfaction and fulfillment. We develop ourselves and others when we take unorganized matter into our hands and mold it into something of beauty" ("Happiness, Your Heritage," 118).

Great creations don't always involve physical beauty or form. One evening our ward Relief Society held a meeting for which each sister was asked to be prepared to talk about or show something she had been learning or working on or creating. Many brought beautiful crafts or handwork to show. Some brought ideas for family activities; one had a clever tip for discarding cooking grease. Finally, it was the turn of a sister who had formerly served as our ward's Relief Society president. She stood up and started with the apology, "I'm not creative." We all immediately objected, knowing the goodness of this sister, her countless works of service, and her humble, kind, and loving demeanor. That is when we realized the injustice of measuring creativity by tangible works. Again, from President Uchtdorf:

"You may think you don't have talents, but that is a false assumption, for we all have talents and gifts, every one of us. The bounds of creativity extend far beyond the limits of a canvas or a sheet of paper and do not require a brush, a pen, or the keys of a piano. Creation means bringing into existence something that did not exist before—colorful gardens, harmonious homes, family memories, flowing laughter.

"What you create doesn't have to be perfect. . . .

"If you still feel incapable of creating, start small. Try to see how many smiles you can create, write a letter of appreciation, learn a new skill, identify a space and beautify it.

"Nearly a century and a half ago, President Brigham Young spoke to the Saints of his day. 'There is a great work for the Saints to do,' he said. 'Progress, and improve upon and make beautiful everything around you. Cultivate the earth, and cultivate your minds. Build cities, adorn your habitations, make gardens, orchards, and vineyards, and render the earth so pleasant that when you look upon your labors you may do so with pleasure, and that angels may delight to come and visit your beautiful locations. In the mean time continually seek to adorn your minds with all the graces of the Spirit of Christ.'

"The more you trust and rely upon the Spirit, the greater your capacity to create. That is your opportunity in this life and your destiny in the life to come . . . trust and rely on the Spirit. As you take the normal opportunities of your daily life and create something of beauty and helpfulness, you improve not only the world around you but also the world within you" ("Happiness, Your Heritage," 119).

Indeed, the most important creations are not beautiful gardens and other physical pro-ductions that will fade and decay. The greatest and most long-lasting creations happen daily, hourly, and even moment by moment. With every righteous choice we make, we sow seeds of eternal life. When we think uplifting thoughts, our spirits blossom and become more attractive. When we choose to exercise faith, repent, and keep a commandment, we are cultivating something that did not exist before. When we serve others, we create gardens of goodness and those blessings that bear fruit in them. If we seek to plant and nourish Christ in our hearts, His Spirit will radiate from us. Thereby, in addition to creating physical beauty, we continually create a spiritual environment. We cultivate light or darkness, loveli-ness or ugliness within ourselves by the thoughts we develop and the influences we choose. Often without fully realizing it, we experience spiritual sight, hearing, taste, smell, and feeling, for our spirit bodies are as real as our temporal bodies. We also radiate a spiritual atmosphere that affects the spiritual senses of those around us. We exert and develop our most godly creative powers when we generate spiritual beauty for others in some way. That is why it brings us so much joy to serve our fellow man.

Just as we may forget that everyday growing things offer a glimpse of the eternal process of creation that is ongoing in this life and the next, we may forget that our everyday choices are also a continual process of creating the world we and others inhabit. So create something beautiful and eternal today—it's in your spiritual DNA to do exactly that.

"AFTER ITS KIND"

One of our favorite things about gardening is that although much effort is required and many factors are involved, you generally know what you are going to get when you plant your garden. Unless you plant the mystery mix seed packet or the pony pack of plants that even the experts at the nursery can't identify, you know that what you sow is what you will reap. Sometimes we have been surprised that what was supposed to be jalapeño peppers really were Hungarian wax peppers or what was supposed to be a 'Big Beef' beefsteak tomato was actually a 'Sweet 100' cherry tomato. That certainly was not the fault of the plants. They had just been mislabeled at the nursery. No doubt you have had your share of garden surprises as well, labeling mistakes that left you with white delphiniums instead of purple. But we have never had the experience of planting a corn seed and harvesting cucumbers instead. Nor have we planted carrots and dug up potatoes. Even though we have always wished that we could plant pansies and get a money tree, it just doesn't work that way. It is a law of nature as predictable as sunrises, sunsets, and the tides of the sea. What you sow, you reap. That is God's decree. At the dawn of Creation, He commanded every living thing to multiply and replenish the earth "after his kind" (Genesis 1:12, 24–25), "whose seed in itself yieldeth its own likeness upon the earth" (Abraham 4:11). The phrase "after their kind" is replete with meaning (Moses 2:21, 24–25; Abraham 4:21, 24–25). It applies not just to animals and agriculture but also to actions and attitudes.

"Be not deceived; God is not mocked," the Apostle Paul declared, "for whatsoever a man soweth, that shall he also reap.

"For he that soweth to his flesh shall of the flesh reap corruption; but he that soweth to the Spirit shall of the Spirit reap life everlasting.

"And let us not be weary in well doing: for in due season we shall reap, if we faint not" (Galatians 6:7–9).

Jesus taught this principle many times during His earthly ministry. In the Sermon on the Mount, the Savior said, "Blessed are the merciful: for they shall obtain mercy" (Matthew 5:7). Later He admonished His disciples, "Judge not unrighteously, that ye be not judged: but judge righteous judgment" (JST Matthew 7:2). Some have called this the principle of reciprocity—what you do comes back to you, whether it be good or evil (in our modern vernacular we say, "What goes around comes around"). In the Book of Mormon, Alma called it the "law of restoration":

"And it is requisite with the justice of God that men should be judged according to their works; and if their works were good in this life, and the desires of their hearts were good, that they should also, at the last day, be restored unto that which is good.

"And if their works are evil they shall be restored unto them for evil. . . .

"The one raised to happiness according to his desires of happiness, or good according to his desires of good; and the other to evil according to his desires of evil; for as he has desired to do evil all the day long even so shall he have his reward of evil when the night cometh" (Alma 41:2–5).

In a way we are planting seeds with every deed and every word. What we harvest—what comes back either to bless or to condemn us, both here and hereafter—will be "after its kind" (Abraham 4:25). If we have planted kindness, we will receive kindness in return. If we have planted righteousness in our hearts and lives and nourished it, we will inevitably reap its delicious fruits. It is an eternal law as fixed and firm as the law we see in nature, according to which both flora and fauna reproduce after their own kind. In our day, the Lord has declared that "intelligence cleaveth unto intelligence; wisdom receiveth wisdom; truth embraceth truth; virtue loveth virtue; light cleaveth unto light; mercy hath compassion on mercy and claimeth her own; justice continueth its course and claimeth its own" (D&C 88:40). Seeds of indolence never will produce intelligence. Neglecting serious scripture study does not produce gospel scholars. Living an immoral life cannot bring virtue, no matter how

much one might wish for it. The kinds of seeds we plant determine the kinds of fruit we enjoy.

This principle applies not only to our own personal lives but also to our parenting. No doubt you have heard the adage, "The apple doesn't fall far from the tree." We often use that saying to mean that a child looks like or acts just like one or both parents. It is tangible evidence of the "after their kind" principle, whether for good or for ill. "A chip off the old block" is a great thing when it is positive—when our daughters are radiantly beautiful and charming like Mom and our sons are handsome and strong like Dad. We are quick to take credit for positive traits and just as quick to blame the other half of the gene pool for any deficiencies we observe. It is downright disconcerting at best and terribly painful at worst when our children become just like us in bad ways, adopting attitudes and actions that we certainly didn't want them to embrace.

Elder Richard L. Evans, of the Quorum of the Twelve Apostles, observed: "Sometimes some parents mistakenly feel that they can relax a little as to conduct and conformity or take perhaps a so called liberal view of basic and fundamental things—thinking that a little laxness or indulgence won't matter—or they may fail to teach or to attend Church, or may voice critical views. Some parents sometimes seem to feel that they can ease up a little on the fundamentals without affecting their family or their family's future. *But if a parent goes a little off course, the children are likely to exceed the parent's example*" (Conference Report, Oct. 1964, 135–36; emphasis added).

That should give us pause. Are we as conscientious about the seeds we are daily planting in the hearts and minds of our children as we are about the quality of seeds we plant in our vegetable gardens? Do we realize that every moment we are planting seeds in the fertile seedbeds of our children's lives? One of the best lessons we have learned from our garden is to continually ask ourselves: "What kind of spiritual fruit do I want to harvest in my life?" "What kind of spiritual seed am I planting right now?" Fortunately, if we find—as we all do at one time or another—that the seeds we are planting and the fruit we desire are not of the same kind, we can stop, dig up, and replant. That works as well for parents as it does for produce, though it doesn't guarantee immediate results.

Several years ago we wrote a book about near-death experiences and spirit world encounters in the context of the revelations of the Restoration. It was fascinating to see how closely such experiences correspond with principles of the gospel. Of particular interest to us was the phenomenon of the life review by which the deceased person came face to face with his or her life. Those who are assessing their mortal lives in this review or self-judgment process

are often blessed with the miraculous ability to perceive and experience how their lives affected other people and other things. "Mine was not a review," one woman remembered, "it was a reliving. For me, it was a reliving of *every* thought I had ever thought, *every* word I had ever spoken, and *every* deed I had ever done; *plus* the effect of each thought, word, and deed on everyone and anyone who had ever come within my environment or sphere of influence" (Atwater, *Coming Back to Life,* 36). That is a sobering thought. In a more literal way than we now comprehend, this agricultural principle of reaping what we have sown not only applies in our earthly lives and relationships, but is fulfilled even more perfectly in our eternal reward. Planting seeds, nourishing seeds, seeing plants scatter their seeds, and harvesting fruits whose seeds are in themselves are all meant to serve as a constant visual reminder from the Creator that we are, more importantly, planting spiritual seeds that are guaranteed to one day produce after their own kind.

LIGHT AND LIFE

Unless you are a mushroom farmer, every plant in your yard and garden needs both sunlight and water. Without them, the plants inevitably die. Each plant may have a different need for light and water—some need a lot of both, and others need only a little—but none of the plants in our garden can survive without both. Through the years we have observed how the plants in our vegetable garden and flower beds exert enormous effort to obtain the light they need, sometimes even twisting and stretching toward the sun. Without adequate light, they cannot grow well and produce their fruit or flowers. We have observed that in a very literal sense, light "giveth life to all things" (D&C 88:13). In like manner, water also gives life. No doubt you have observed how a spring rain can cause a brown, seemingly lifeless lawn to turn green and vibrant almost overnight. It always amazes us to see how some plants can be wilted nearly to the point of no return only to spring back to life with a welcome drink of water. When our family lived in Israel, we observed this remarkable transformation in a most dramatic way. For much of the year the Judean hills surrounding Jerusalem are barren and brown. When we saw sheep and goats in the fields, we wondered what they were grazing on because there appeared to be no living plants. Mark Twain observed the same thing on his visit to the Holy Land and concluded that Judean goats eat rocks! (see *Innocents Abroad*, 208–9). During the space of just a few weeks in the spring, however, those apparently lifeless hills become nearly as lush and green as their counterparts in Ireland. The desert literally blossoms as a rose, its hills and vales magically transformed into a carpet of colorful wildflowers. To us, the phrase "living waters" became much more than a symbolic scriptural term. It was reality.

People, like plants, also need light and water to have life. Light deprivation can have serious side effects, both physically and emotionally. Likewise, dehydration can cause nausea, dizziness, headaches, and even more seriously, organ failure and death. Water and light are just as essential to human growth and productivity as they are to plants. No wonder the Savior used these terms so often to refer to Himself. "I am the light of the world," He declared (John 8:12), and the "fountain of living waters" (Jeremiah 17:13; see John 4:13–14; 7:37–38; Revelation 7:17; D&C 10:66). He is truly the Light that gives life—both temporally and spiritually. "He that followeth me shall not walk in darkness," the Savior taught, "but shall have the *light of life*" (John 8:12;

emphasis added). He is the Living Water that quenches spiritual thirst and gives life—the abundant life (see John 10:10)—when we feel emotionally drained and spiritually wilted, and our lives seem like a barren wasteland. He is the "still waters" by which we can obtain peace in a hectic, stressful life and rest when we are world-weary (Psalm 23:2).

Spiritual Photosynthesis

Sunlight is required for photosynthesis, the process by which plants produce life-giving food for their sustenance, growth, and productivity. In a similar manner, there is a spiritual photosynthesis in humans, a spiritual process by which we are sustained and strengthened and transformed. The Apostle Paul taught that through the Savior's Atonement we become "alive unto God through Jesus Christ our Lord" (Romans 6:11). As the Light of the World and the Fountain of Living Waters, the Savior invites each of us to partake of His life-giving Atonement and experience spiritual photosynthesis—a very real transformation in which the natural man becomes a "new creature in Christ" (2 Corinthians 5:17). That "mighty change" in us is as literal and remarkable as photosynthesis is in plants (Alma 5:14). The "newness of life" that it brings includes a change of heart "that we have no more disposition to do evil, but to do good continually" (Romans 6:4; Mosiah 5:2). Not only do eyes that have been opened by the Light of the World see Him more clearly but with charity—"the pure love of Christ" (Moroni 7:47)—they also see the world around them in a new light.

President Joseph F. Smith described his own experience with spiritual photosynthesis this way:

"The feeling that came upon me was that of pure peace, of love and light. I felt as if I wanted to do good everywhere to everybody and to everything. I felt a newness of life, a newness of desire to do that which was right. There was not one particle of desire for evil left in my soul" (*Gospel Doctrine*, 96).

"I Am the Vine, Ye Are the Branches"

Along our back fence we planted several grapevines. They are a perfect illustration of plants that need light and life to produce fruit. There are Concord grapes for juice, and seedless grapes for eating—green ones, red ones, and black ones. (We even get raisins from them if we forget to pick them in the fall!) If you haven't seen or grown grapevines, you might not know that the vine begins as a cane or branch that is trained to grow upright from the roots, thickening over a few years into a heavy, gnarled, bark-covered trunk. Though it is more like the size of a young tree branch, it takes on the wonderful shape and texture of an old twisted tree. In the spring it is pruned back severely—all of the previous year's canes are cut off—and it looks like a gnarled old piece of deadwood stuck to the fence. It is hard to imagine that anything green could come from it, especially as it remains starkly dormant after many other plants are at the height of their springtime splendor. But finally, in late spring, bright green new branches or shoots begin to form on the wizened old growth. We have trained the scaffolding of branches to grow along wires stretched across the fence. Before long they are growing vigorously in every direction and need some taming. We prune off the branches that are not producing fruit, leaving just enough leaves to capture sunlight for photosynthesis and not so many that the plant creates too much shade for itself. By midsummer the branches are heavily laden with clusters of grapes beginning to take shape on the new growth. Continual pruning is necessary to direct the nourishment to those branches. By autumn the fruits are full and rich with color as they sweeten and grow ripe in the cool nights and warm autumn days, abiding in the vine until the time of their harvest is come (see John 15:4).

Like our Savior in His mortal ministry, that old vine has "no apparent beauty that man should him desire" (*Hymns*, no. 175), but it is the transmitter of life-giving moisture and nourishment for the branches that will form the fruit. The branches only thrive and produce between the vine and the sunlight—the Life and the Light. So powerful is this metaphor that the Lord Himself used it to teach His disciples: "As the branch cannot bear fruit of itself, except it abide in the vine; no more can ye, except ye abide in me. I am the vine, ye are the branches: He that abideth in me, and I in him, the same bringeth forth much fruit: *for without me ye can do nothing*" (John 15:4–5; emphasis added).

Not only is the Savior the Light and Life of the world in very literal ways but He is also the Source of our own individual strength. His power can become

our power. We, the branches, cannot take root and grow and produce eternal works on our own. We are a part of the body of Christ. His power, His sustenance, and His atoning sacrifice make possible our very existence here on earth, the very fruits we bear, and our eternal life. That is what His grace—His redemptive mercy and His perfect love—does *for* us and *to* us. "My grace is sufficient for thee" were the Lord's comforting words to Paul as he struggled with his "thorn in the flesh" (2 Corinthians 12:9, 7). As Paul came to experience the sustaining power of Christ's grace in a personal and powerful way, he declared: "I can do all things through Christ which strengtheneth me" (Philippians 4:13).

"It is through the grace of the Lord Jesus, made possible by his atoning sacrifice . . . that individuals, through faith in the atonement of Jesus Christ and repentance of their sins, receive strength and assistance to do good works that they otherwise would not be able to maintain if left to their own means. This grace is an enabling power that allows men and women to lay hold on eternal life and exaltation after they have expended their own best efforts" (Bible Dictionary, s.v. "Grace," 697).

Thus, the seed Alma urged us to plant in faith can only be nourished by abiding in Christ because, except we are cleansed, pruned, and nourished by *His* love and mercy, our fruit is a transitory illusion. Unless we remain one *with* Him and one *in* Him and He *in us*, our efforts are in vain. They will vanish in the burning. "If a man abide not in me, he is cast forth as a branch, and is withered; and men gather them, and cast them into the fire, and they are burned" (John 15:6).

Each day as we walk past our grapevines, we are reminded that Christ is indeed the "true vine" (John 15:1), the source of our strength, the light of our lives, and the living waters that quench spiritual thirst. Just as plant life cannot be sustained without light and water, our lives cannot be sustained, in the truest sense of the word, without Him. We can no more become what we are intended to become without His grace than grape branches can produce fruit without the vine and the sunlight. Truly, He is the Light of Life.

BLOOM WHERE YOU ARE PLANTED

There is a familiar saying that perhaps you too have heard a zillion times: Bloom where you are planted. It may sound trite, but it is indeed wise counsel. Master gardeners always know the right location to plant trees, flowers, and vegetables. Good, obedient plants always know what they are supposed to do then—bloom where they are planted. Unfortunately, not all of us are master gardeners, and so we end up planting shade plants in full sun and tropical, humidity-loving plants in dry, desert landscapes. Likewise, we ourselves are not always good, obedient plants. Sometimes we don't bloom where we are planted, even when the soil and climate should be to our liking and conducive to our growth. From gardening we have learned a valuable gospel lesson: Our Heavenly Father knows us so perfectly that He plants us in places and circumstances that can bring about our greatest growth and result in our greatest good. When we really understand this principle and truly trust Him, we will indeed bloom where He plants us. Though our seedbeds and blooms may differ, the Master Gardener intends that His children fill the measure of their creation and realize their divine potential.

The Old Testament prophet Isaiah captured this concept with a botanical metaphor recorded in Isaiah 28. Isaiah describes how the farmer (Heavenly Father) plants the seeds

(His children) in various parts of the field (the world). He knows precisely which seeds will do best in which locations of the field. Because the various kinds of seeds have their own individual characteristics and needs, they are likewise planted in individual ways—all for the ultimate growth and productivity of each seed. Clearly Isaiah is teaching us that our loving Heavenly Father knows each of us so well that He sent us to earth at the exact time, in the precise location, and under the specific circumstances that would best help us maximize our divine potential and fulfill our foreordained mission (see Ball and Winn, *Making Sense of Isaiah*, 79–85).

When we really believe that the Lord is not only mindful of us—our challenges, our circumstances, and our individual needs—but has actually placed us in the setting that would yield our greatest growth, we can exercise greater faith in Him and trust in His purposes for us. With such trust, we can then be, as the Apostle Paul admonished, "content with such things as [we] have: for [the Lord] hath said, I will never leave thee, nor forsake thee" (Hebrews 13:5). Alma yearned for greater capacity and power to proclaim the gospel as a "trump of God" so as to "shake the earth," yet he trusted in God's purposes and recognized that he "ought to be content with the things which the Lord hath allotted unto me" (Alma 29:1, 3). Some things we have no control over, and others we do. That which we cannot control is what the Lord has allotted unto us. Finding peace, purpose, and contentment within that allotment is one of life's greatest challenges and one of the requirements of devoted discipleship. The Apostle Paul described such spiritual contentment as "godliness with contentment" (1 Timothy 6:6). "Such contentment is more than shoulder-shrugging passivity," Elder Neal A. Maxwell eloquently declared. "It reflects our participative assent rather than uncaring resignation.

"The Lord knows our circumstances and the intents of our hearts, and surely the talents and gifts He has given us. He is able to gauge perfectly how we have performed within what is allotted to us, including by lifting up some of the many hands that hang down. Thus, yearning for expanded opportunities while failing to use those at hand is bad form spiritually. . . .

"Thus, within our allotments

we see how the saintly display kindness even within barbed-wire circumstances, yet others have barbed-wire attitudes even within opulence. Meanwhile, the discontented continue to build their own pools of self-pity, some Olympic size. . . .

"When spiritually aligned, a poise can come, even when we do not know 'the meaning of all things' (1 Ne. 11:17). Such contented assurance produces not arrogance but quiet acceptance, which is its own form of being 'anxiously engaged' but without all the bells and whistles (D&C 58:27–28).

"However, this spiritual contentment rests on our accepting the Atonement of Jesus, because we 'have come to a knowledge of the goodness of God, and his matchless power, and his wisdom, and his patience, and his long-suffering towards the children of men; and also, the atonement which has been prepared from the foundation of the world' (Mosiah 4:6)" (Maxwell, "Content with the Things Allotted unto Us," 72).

We have had the privilege of visiting some of the most beautiful gardens in the world. It seems that with every visit we find a plant that we covet and desire to have in our own garden. Unfortunately, we tend to covet those trees and flowers that grow well in an environment much different from our own. We have learned, often by sad experience, that some of the most beautiful tropical flowers and delectable fruits from the islands just won't survive in Utah with its harsh, killing-frost winters and hot, dry summers. Likewise, some of our favorite plants, such as rhododendrons, azaleas, hydrangeas, and dogwoods, thrive in acidic soils but die in the alkaline Utah Valley soil. Other plants require cool, wet weather. We lived in Arizona for several years and fell in love with saguaro and other varieties of cacti and desert flora. But no matter how much we love them and want to grow them, they just won't survive in our yard. It's a fact of life—you can't grow a rain forest in a desert, and vice versa. We can grumble and complain about it and go to extraordinary efforts and expense to fight against nature, or we can be content with that which the Lord has allotted and improve upon that. We have discovered in our gardening that covetousness never satisfies. When we obsess about the grass that is greener on the other side of the fence, when we covet our neighbor's beautiful gardens and water features, we end up dissatisfied with our garden, with its own beautiful flowers and bounteous fruits and vegetables.

In our lives, as well as our gardens, the lack of godliness with contentment leaves us unfulfilled, frustrated, and discouraged. Divine content, on the other hand, gives us not only a sense of spiritual satisfaction but also profound gratitude for what the Lord has allotted, which in turn prods us to do a little more and to be a little better. We will want to bloom a little brighter if we remember that we are anxiously engaged in the very thing we longed for—even fought for—before we ever came to earth. We are participants in the great plan of salvation. We "shouted for joy" at the prospect of such participation (Job 38:7). "We knew before we were born that we were coming to earth for bodies and experience and that we would have joys and sorrows, ease and pain, comforts and hardships, health and sickness, successes and disappointments, and we knew also that after a period of life we would die," President Spencer W. Kimball taught. "We accepted these eventualities with a glad heart, eager to accept both the favorable and unfavorable. We eagerly accepted the chance to come earthward even though it might be for only a day or a year. Perhaps we were not so much concerned whether we should die of disease, of accident, or of senility. We were willing

to take life as it came and as we might organize and control it, and this without murmur, complaint, or unreasonable demands" (Kimball, *Faith Precedes the Miracle*, 106).

We can't control where we are planted, how we are planted, or what the garden down the street looks like, but we can continue to bloom in our own flower bed of life without "murmur, complaint, or unreasonable demands," as President Kimball reminded us. We can bloom by repenting, loving, serving, and seeking to bring blooms into the lives of others whose allotment in life may be less than our own. That is what godliness with contentment and blooming where we are planted are really all about.

WEED WHACKING

Weeds are part of our mortal existence, albeit the bane of any gardener's existence. It has been so since God declared to Adam and Eve that thorns, thistles, and all kinds of noxious weeds would afflict and torment them (see Genesis 3:17–18). Even as our first parents were afflicted and tormented by weeds, so are we today, and for the very same reason. It is interesting that even with all of the scientific and technological advances through the centuries, weeds have not been eradicated from the world. We may perhaps have better means for their control, but we must still deal with them. And that is not all bad. People, as well as gardens, become better with more effective weed control. Our lives, like our flower beds and vegetable gardens, need to be consistently weeded of those things that not only are unsightly but can also choke out the good by robbing us of the needed nutrients of life (see Matthew 13:22). Every good gardener knows that there are two important dimensions of weed control—eradication and prevention. Both are needed for spiritual weed control in one's soul as well.

Weed Eradication

One of the things we appreciated most when we came home from presiding over a mission was the freedom to work in our yard and garden. There isn't much time or opportunity to do that when you are living in a mission home and almost every moment of the day and night is taken up with mission responsibilities. So it was very therapeutic to return to our gardening activities. If therapy was not enough motivation, the yard and garden themselves had been somewhat neglected for three years and were in need of attention. Within a few weeks after our arrival home from our mission, things were at least back on the road to how they were before we left. While Brent was working in the vegetable garden a couple of months later, our daughter Tiffany, who, along with her husband and children, had lived in our home while we were away, asked, "Why don't you have big weeds in the garden like we had?" Brent replied, "I don't let them get big." That is a great lesson for spiritual weed control in our lives. Sins and bad habits are like weeds. They start out small, and if not eradicated early, they will cause all kinds of problems and become increasingly more difficult to get rid of as they grow.

We have often thought how insidious it is that many weeds look much the same as good plants when they start out. We are sometimes lulled into thinking everything in the garden is fine, and we let up a little on our weed-pulling vigilance. If we aren't careful, the weeds will take over the garden in a short time. Some weeds disguise themselves with pretty flowers and foliage. We are fooled into thinking they are good plants, too pretty to pull out. Then, instead of pretty flowers, they produce thorns and stickers of all kinds—noxious weeds that truly afflict and torment us. Likewise, weeds tend to grow as close to the good plants as they can. Even if you recognize them as weeds, it is still difficult to eliminate them without hurting the good plants. It is especially tricky to get rid of emerging weeds in such crops as carrots, which start out very small and delicate. Often the only way you can eliminate weeds in crops like these is to get down on your hands and knees and pluck out by hand the weeds that have intermingled with the good plants. Getting rid of weeds when they are small and refusing to let up are the keys.

In the New Testament the Savior gave the parable of the wheat and the tares (see Matthew 13:24–30, 36–42) in which the burning of the tares represents the destruction of the wicked at His Second Coming, but there are other applications as well. The word *tares* is not one we use that much today. Some Bible scholars have called tares "bastard wheat" because they look much like wheat—until they are almost ready to be harvested. If mistaken for wheat and consumed, tares can make a person violently ill. These wily weeds can also represent temptations and sins that seem harmless, almost appearing good, at the outset but rob our souls of spiritual nutrition—guidance toward good and the discernment of evil that comes with the companionship of the Holy Ghost. And like weeds, if they are not nipped in the bud and eradicated while small through repentance and increased obedience to the principles of the gospel, they will become larger and larger—more serious and more difficult to abandon. Unlike the man in the parable (who represents the Savior), we cannot wait until the harvest to eliminate tares from our own lives. Procrastinating repentance and the abandonment of bad habits allows their roots to grow deeper and deeper. In our flower beds and vegetable gardens, we should watch for and pull up weeds as soon as they appear. In our lives we need to do the same. Fortunately the Lord has given us the sacrament each week as a time to renew our covenants and to weed our lives of those things that are stunting our spiritual growth. That sacred, sacramental ordinance, if properly understood and used, helps us eliminate the spiritual weeds in our lives while they are yet small.

There is something else that is essential to know about eradication of weeds, whether eradicating noxious and undesirable plants in the garden or overcoming noxious sins and bad habits in our lives that afflict and torment: You must get to the roots. We learned this the hard way. We purchased a chemical weed killer that was on sale. We thought it was a great deal, because it promised effective control at much less expense and in less time than the weed killer we ordinarily used. At first the new weed killer appeared to work well. The weeds turned brown and died almost immediately. To our horror, however, the weeds reappeared almost as quickly as they had died. What was going on? We discovered that the bargain weed killer merely burned the foliage of the weed but did nothing to the roots. It had an immediate cosmetic effect, but it really wasn't doing anything to eliminate the undesirable plant. What we needed was a systemic weed killer—a chemical that is absorbed by the foliage and goes directly to the roots—to kill the whole plant from roots to leaves. Likewise, it is not enough just to mow down the weeds that may appear in our lawn. It may look great for a day or two, but dandelions and other weeds inevitably show their ugly heads again. You have to get to the roots!

Spiritually speaking, it works the same in our lives. We cannot just cut back, mow down, or cosmetically hide our sins. Any attempt to only superficially weed our souls of sin will fail unless we use a spiritual systemic that gets to the root of the problem. Repentance must be comprehensive, not cosmetic. Living the gospel is not about show. It is about what we are to our very core. Self-help gimmicks and our own limited efforts at self-control may have a temporary effect, but only Jesus Christ, through His atoning sacrifice, activated by our fervent faith in Him, can reach into our roots and change our hearts—our very being.

Weed Prevention

Equally important to weed eradication is weed prevention. We have learned that the best way to ensure a weed-free lawn is to ensure that the grass is healthy and growing vigorously. Have you ever noticed that if there is a spot in your lawn that is stressed for whatever reason—bugs, a lack of water, or damage done by the lawnmower—weeds start to appear where they had not been when the lawn was healthy? Likewise, if our flower beds are filled with good strong flowers and shrubs, there is less room for weeds to thrive. The greater the

overall health and vigor of the garden, the fewer weeds there will be. An ounce of prevention is worth a pound of cure is true in the garden as well as in matters of health.

In another parable in the New Testament, Jesus taught the principle that real repentance and spiritual well-being is not determined solely by the absence of sin, but rather by the filling of one's life with an abundance of faith, worthy living, and service to God and fellowmen. It is not enough simply to cleanse a filthy vessel, but rather, the cleansed vessel must then be filled with a pure substance so that it cannot again be defiled (see Alma 60:23).

"When the unclean spirit is gone out of a man, he walketh through dry places, seeking rest; and finding none, he saith, I will return unto my house whence I came out.

"And when he cometh, he findeth it swept and garnished.

"Then goeth he, and taketh to him seven other spirits more wicked than himself; and they enter in, and dwell there: and the last state of that man is worse than the first" (Luke 11:24–26).

We could replace the word "house" in the parable with "garden," and the words "swept and garnished" with "weeded," and the principle would be the same. Although our garden (our life) is weeded or cleansed, we remain vulnerable to a reinvasion of all manner of temptations and trouble if our lives are not filled up with renewed acts of righteousness and greater devotion to God. When our lives are spiritually healthy—filled with faithfulness and righteous desires and deeds—there is less room for sin to take root. "Do not try merely to *discard* a bad habit or a bad thought," taught President Boyd K. Packer of the Quorum of the Twelve. "*Replace* it. When you try to eliminate a bad habit, if the spot where it used to be is left open it will sneak back and crawl again into that empty space. It grew there; it will struggle to stay there. When you discard it, fill up the spot where it was. Replace it with something good. Replace it with unselfish thoughts, with unselfish acts. Then, if an evil habit or addiction tries to return, it will have to fight for attention. . . . You are in charge of you. I repeat, it is very, very difficult to eliminate a bad habit [or sin] just by trying to discard it. Replace it" (*Mine Errand from the Lord,* 175).

In our lives, as in our gardens, there will be far fewer weeds to whack down if our faith is being fed continually and our spiritual life is growing vigorously. As President Ezra Taft Benson taught, "It is better to prepare and prevent than to repair and repent" (*Teachings of Ezra Taft Benson,* 285). Keeping our souls healthy and vigorous through daily scripture study and prayer, by consistently keeping the commandments and serving God and our fellowmen prevents a multitude of sins. Spiritual weakness always invites sin, just as a weakened and stressed garden will always be invaded by weeds.

Thus sins, like weeds, will always creep up on us and attempt to grow in our minds and souls. We, like gardeners, usually don't know the weeds have been planted until we see them sprout. The real test is in what we do with them when we recognize them. Repentance is the best spiritual weed whacker and good spiritual health is the best weed (sin) preventer.

DON'T SPRAY ROUNDUP
ON YOUR TOMATOES

We love flowers. We love vegetables. We love fruit. We love trees. That is why we are avid gardeners. But please don't ask us which is our favorite. That is like asking which grandchild is our favorite. If, however, we were forced to choose one item in our garden that we just couldn't live without (and even that scenario seems impossible), it would probably be tomatoes. There is nothing like a ripe, juicy, homegrown tomato. We call them garden candy in our family. We endure store-bought, tasteless-by-comparison tomatoes in the winter as we longingly look forward to picking more garden candy in the summer. Our mouths are watering just thinking about them!

As much as we love tomatoes, they are not always easy to grow. At times we have harvested bounteously, and at other times our appetite for a big, juicy, sweet tomato has gone unsatisfied. There are pests to deal with each year—great big ugly green caterpillars that love to eat tomato plants. There are soil-borne viruses and curly top to worry about. Sometimes there is drought and water rationing, which tomato plants really, really dislike. Then there is the heat. Tomatoes won't develop if it is too hot at a critical time in the growing season. It is tough to grow tomatoes. It takes a lot of effort. And that is probably another reason why we cherish homegrown tomatoes as we do.

While Brent was presiding over a mission, we didn't have a garden. Not just because we were busy but also because the mission home was surrounded by large trees that blocked much of the sunshine that a good garden requires. There was a spot, however, in a back flower bed where we thought a tomato plant might grow. The location and other conditions were not ideal but nonetheless worth the effort, we thought. We planted and watched as the plant grew. It didn't thrive, but we worked with it and cultivated around it, fertilized it, and babied it—it was the only thing that remotely resembled a garden. Soon the blossoms transformed into small green tomatoes. With our mouths watering, we waited and watched. The green tomatoes turned to orange and then to red. One day after a long day of meetings, we returned home to harvest a big, beautiful tomato to enjoy at dinner. When Brent went around to the back to pick his prize tomato, it wasn't there. It was gone. All of the tomatoes were gone, along with most of the plant. Something (probably a deer, raccoon, or another animal that lived in the woods behind the mission home) had gotten to it before we had. We had worked, watched, weeded, waited, and worked some more to be able to have some garden candy. Now it was all gone. We were devastated. You would have thought a loved one had died. No vine-ripened tomatoes? Perish the thought! Was life still worth living? We're exaggerating, of course. But it is indeed discouraging when you put so much work into something that you desire and that brings you great satisfaction only to have it ruined or lost through no fault of your own.

In light of what we have told you about our passion for vine-ripened, homegrown tomatoes, can you imagine us watering, weeding, and working in our garden for weeks and months, only to carelessly stomp on the plants and smash the ripe tomatoes? Or just as the plants are growing most vigorously, and the prospects of a great harvest are the highest, can you see us spraying Roundup (an herbicide that is intended to kill weeds and unwanted plants) on our prized tomatoes? Of course not! How ridiculous! No one who loves a tomato would thoughtlessly or purposely do something that would destroy it. As we have worked in our garden through the years, we have learned that we would never, ever consider doing that temporally, but we often do it spiritually.

We refer to Alma's example, or "experiment" (Alma 32:27), that illustrates how faith is developed and how, if properly nurtured, it will ultimately yield the fruits of God's love—eternal life. We plant the seed of faith after hearing "the word of God" and choosing to act upon it (Romans 10:17). We cultivate it with prayer, scripture study, service, attendance at our church meetings, and keeping the commandments. We weed it by repentance. We protect it by seeking the guidance of the Spirit. As we do so, our faith grows and our bosom swells, as Alma describes it (see Alma 32:28). Our personal spirituality and capacity increase. As we continue this process, we taste the fruits of the gospel and we are transformed slowly but surely into new creatures in Christ with even greater faith and strength (see 2 Corinthians 5:17). "Faith is a gift of God bestowed as a reward for personal righteousness," Elder Bruce R. McConkie taught. "It is always given when righteousness is present, and the greater the measure of obedience to God's laws the greater will be the endowment of faith" (*Doctrinal New Testament Commentary*, 3:391). And, we could add, the greater the endowment of faith, the greater the fruits that we will experience in our lives and be able to share with others through our service.

So why do we often, when our faith is in flower, expose ourselves to people, situations, and influences that are intended to destroy or degrade it? Why do we often go days and weeks without watering our faith, when we would never withhold water from our plants if we wanted to harvest fruit or enjoy flowers? If cultivating our faith requires devotion, righteousness, and repentance, then spiritual slothfulness and exposure to sinful influences destroy what we've cultivated. It is like spraying spiritual Roundup on our faith, our testimonies, and the very fruits of the gospel we desire to enjoy in their fullness. We would never spray Roundup on our precious tomatoes. Why then would we do something even more destructive to that which is infinitely more valuable than a homegrown tomato?

During our mission, we often marveled at the miracle of testimonies taking root in the hearts of converts as they were nourished by our missionaries. Too often we then watched with increasing dismay as many of those converts failed to nourish and protect their newly found faith when the missionaries moved on.

Sometimes they would return to former associates and environments that drove away the Spirit. They might gradually stop attending Church meetings. Other times they would listen to enemies of the Church or read anti-Mormon literature designed specifically to wither tender shoots of faith. A testimony, as President Harold B. Lee once said, is "as fragile as an orchid" and "as elusive as a moonbeam" (*Teachings of*

Harold B. Lee, 139). It must be guarded and watched over jealously. We need to diligently and consistently look at how we are either nourishing or destroying our faith every day. When we're tempted to knowingly expose ourselves to Spirit-alienating influences, to sin, to spiritually slack off, or to forget what's really at stake, we could stop and ask ourselves, "Am I spraying Roundup on my tomatoes?" But the real question should be, "Is this sin or this negative influence—this thing that I desire at this moment—really worth losing my hard-won spiritual growth or even risking the loss of all that I desire most?"

Unfortunately, there have been times when we have accidently sprayed Roundup on desirable plants because we didn't take steps to protect them. It was not intentional, but the result was the same. We learned quickly that when the herbicide has been administered and absorbed, there is nothing we can do to save the plant. Regrettably, all we can do is watch it wither and die, a frustrating, irreversible consequence of our lack of diligence. In contrast to carelessly spraying our plants, spiritual Roundup in our lives (or alienating the Spirit) is rarely accidental, but it can be reversed. The singed or sickly plant that is our soul can be healed because the Lord is not only the Great Gardener but the Great Healer, reviving the wilted, replacing the dead, dry, and ugly growth in our lives with beautiful blooms. Even if we, spiritually speaking, do something as stupid and destructive as spraying Roundup on prized tomatoes, all is not lost. There can yet be the exquisite deliciousness of the desired fruit of the tree of life, if we seek to eliminate the spiritual Roundup of our lives, passionately protecting and consistently nourishing the prized seed lovingly planted within our hearts.

INFINITE IN VARIETY,
UNIFIED IN PURPOSE

One of the most difficult problems a gardener faces is choosing from among the many varieties of plants and seeds at the local greenhouse. The dilemma is often not what to plant where but not having room to plant everything! One thing that helps narrow down the choices is the fact that each plant has specific uses, features, and strengths as well as limitations and drawbacks. No one plant has all possible desirable attributes. None is perfect in every way. Obviously, some plants produce foods, fibers, medicines, and other products useful to man while others are desirable for their beauty, shade, or protection. The differences are what make them all work together to create a beautiful, bounteous, and beneficial earth. If one plant was perfect and could do everything, others would not be needed, but the world would be mind-numbingly monotonous. That each plant has its own unique contribution means that each is needed, and harmony prevails.

From observing the world around us, we can see that God loves variety, growth, and differentiation, and He abhors monotony, stagnation, and sameness. There is infinite diversity in all the things He created. Botanists and biologists are still discovering new species of plants and animals. All living things are made to evolve and grow continually, adapting to their changing circumstances. We can learn a great deal about ourselves and about others by looking at the multiplicity that God has ordained in nature.

Brent loves flowering plants of all kinds. Though Wendy also loves flowers, she is usually attracted to the foliage of a plant first. What will it look like before and after it has finished flowering? Color is important, but so is texture and shape. Placing two or three plants, each with leaves of different colors, textures, and shapes, in close proximity may cause them all to enhance one another. Height, width, and shape of plants are more important than we may think, and we often forget to take these factors into account. They help direct the eye to the focal point of the yard or house. All of these factors are essential to consider when creating a harmonious, useful, and functioning landscape. Even where plants grow wild, variety adds power and beauty. Mother Nature, in her seeming randomness, is actually the best

landscape architect of all. President Brigham Young spoke of the importance and influence of beauty and variety in nature as well as in people.

"Let the people bring out their talents, and have the variety within them brought forth and made manifest so that we can behold it, like the variety in the works of nature. See the variety God has created—no two trees alike, no two leaves, no two spears of grass alike. The same variety that we see in all the works of God, that we see in the features, visages and forms, exists in the spirits of men. Now let us develop the variety within us, and show to the world that we have talent and taste, and prove to the heavens that our minds are set on beauty and true excellence, so that we can become worthy to enjoy the society of angels, and raise ourselves above the level of the wicked world and begin to increase in faith, and the power that God has given us, and to show to the world an example worthy of imitation" (*Discourses*, 424).

Our middle daughter imagined for years that she was in the shadow of her older and younger sisters. She felt that they were both more attractive than she and that both had outwardly visible performing talents. She struggled for years, trying to find an art or sport or activity she could excel in without competing with her sisters. She fretted over her appearance and thought that if she could pick the right outfit or get

the right hairstyle, she would finally be beautiful. You know how this so-called ugly duckling story turns out. As Tiffany went on with her life, trying to be righteous, marrying, having children, and serving in the Church, her true talents and abilities began to emerge. Though they are not necessarily the same talents as her sisters', they are very real talents that bless the lives of many. She is a wonderful, true friend, a supportive and inspiring wife, and a thoughtful, loving daughter. She has learned the art of being balanced and content as a stay-at-home mother, always putting her family first. She teaches her children the gospel and good manners. As she has developed these talents through her service, a kind of grace and beauty has enveloped her. Her life has sprouted, unfolded, and blossomed into the creation she was intended to be.

Heavenly Father delights in the variety of His children and is disappointed when we reject our individuality by trying to be exact replicas of each other or of some vainly promoted ideal model. If we were all alike, most of us would not be needed or appreciated. Sameness causes us to miss our singular purpose and the joy of being useful. Under such homogeny the world would be stagnant and could not fulfill the measure of its creation. There would be no need to sacrifice selfishness in order to become unified because we would already be so uniform. How drab, dull, and depressing our existence would be! Variety and uniqueness in individuals are the fruits of our sacred and blessed agency. They are a source of personal and collective eternal surprise and endless delight. Let each of us do our part to beautify and unify the landscape of the Lord by seeking out and embracing our distinctive identity while blooming within the bounds of the Lord's purposes.

A WISE AND LOVING GARDENER

Wendy loves to prune—to lop off lanky, ungainly branches, get rid of dead under-growth, and tame and reshape some of our overgrown "babies." But she has a hard time stopping there. She has been known to become so obsessed with cleaning up a bush or a tree with a set of pruning shears that Brent has to stage an intervention. She can always see something else that could be sheared back a little more closely. Perfection evades her, but that doesn't keep her from trying. She is, when it comes to pruning, like a movie star addicted to plastic surgery.

There is a science to pruning. You need to know which plants to prune and when to prune them, how much to prune, and where to prune. If you want to stop growth on a branch, you must make a cut on the stem between the growth buds. If you want to encour-age branching, you should cut off the stem between two small branches. If you want to create one new branch, you should cut at an angle—or something like that. We confess that we really don't know because we haven't cared enough to study and learn it. We just like the feeling of trimming things up. We rarely know which, when, where, how much, or even why. We don't even worry about whether our pruners are sharp; we just pull until the

61

branch comes off. Most of our "babies" are tough enough to take it, but when one doesn't make it, we just replace it with something tougher.

We have often thought how thankful we are that the Lord is an expert, eternal Gardener who knows perfectly how to prune *His* "babies." Pruning is absolutely essential for certain plants (and people) if you love and care about them and want them to achieve their full potential and better serve your purposes. Such trimming shapes and strengthens and beautifies. It directs growth to create bigger and better fruit and flower production. Cutting back

also protects a plant from growth in places and in ways that would cause damage to it or other plants around it. It gets rid of useless and even harmful dead growth that robs parts of the plant of the awakening light of the sun. New growth can then sprout in places that have never seen life. So, too, can Heavenly Father shape and fit His children, not only to be useful and experience maximum growth and blessing in this life but also to become beautiful, perfected, and exalted in His own celestial garden.

The same principles apply to thinning fruits, vegetables, and flower bulbs. It may seem at first that a thick growth of carrot sprouts or an apple tree heavily laden with many blossoms or developing fruits promises a bounteous harvest, but in reality the sunlight, water, nutrition, and space available to the plant means the actual fruits will be small, weak, and perhaps even deformed or useless. Some of the sprouts or fruits have to be removed in order that others may have ample room and provision to grow to their optimum useful size. Likewise, it is encouraging to think that a few flower bulbs will multiply into many, but eventually they grow too crowded to produce vigorous flowers. They have to be dug up and divided every few years, or there will be too much competition for available resources. A wise gardener knows how many apples a tree can bear and how much space a carrot needs to grow. He knows how to separate and transplant bulbs for optimum results. The greatest Gardener knows we cannot be or do all things. He knows perfectly our individual needs and purposes. He knows what has to go and what should be kept in order for us to be fruitful and accomplish our mission. He knows when it is time to transplant us and exactly where we will blossom best. If we fail to trust Him and yield to His perfectly practiced hand, we will end up producing weak, useless, or distorted fruit and thereby, perhaps, deprive others of opportunities to become all that they could be

In a classic parable entitled "The Gardener and the Currant Bush," President Hugh B. Brown told the story of a time in his life when he was pruned back and chastened by the Lord. He likened himself and the rest of us to God's "babies" who don't understand the severe trimmings and transplantings we must often endure:

"In the early dawn, a young gardener was pruning his trees and shrubs. He had one choice currant bush which had gone too much to wood. He feared therefore that it would produce little, if any, fruit.

"Accordingly, he trimmed and pruned the bush and cut it back. In fact, when he had finished, there was little left but stumps and roots.

"Tenderly he considered what was left. It looked so sad and deeply hurt. On every stump there seemed to be a tear where the pruning knife had cut away the growth of early spring. The poor bush seemed to speak to him, and he thought he heard it say:

"'Oh, how could you be so cruel to me; you who claim to be my friend, who planted me and cared for me when I was young, and nurtured and encouraged me to grow? Could you not see that I was rapidly responding to your care? I was nearly half as large as the trees across the fence, and might soon have become like one of them. But now you've cut my branches back; the green, attractive leaves are gone, and I am in disgrace among my fellows.'

"The young gardener looked at the weeping bush and heard its plea with sympathetic understanding. His voice was full of kindness as he said, 'Do not cry; what I have done to you was necessary that you might be a prize currant bush in my garden. You were not intended to give shade or shelter by your branches. My purpose when I planted you was that you should bear fruit. When I want currants, a tree, regardless of its size, cannot supply the need.

"'No, my little currant bush, if I had allowed you to continue to grow as you had started, all your strength would have gone to wood; your roots would not have gained a firm hold, and the purpose for which I brought you into my garden would have been defeated.

Your place would have been taken by another, for you would have been barren. You must not weep; all this will be for your own good; and some day, when you see more clearly, when you are richly laden with luscious fruit, you will thank me and say, "Surely, he was a wise and loving gardener. He knew the purpose of my being, and I thank him now for what I then thought was cruelty"'" (Brown, *Eternal Quest*, 243–44).

Whenever we prune, thin, or transplant, we find ourselves thinking of this parable and mentally console our newly diminished trees, bushes, and other "babies." At the same time we cannot help but hear the echoes of the Lord's voice in our ears as we recall painful and poignant memories of our own moments of chastening. Then we, like the parable's currant bush, are compelled to thank the Gardener for the pruning that once seemed unbearable and even unthinkable but always ended up producing greater happiness and growth than we were capable of imagining.

NEW GROWTH

One of the most exciting sights for an avid gardener is seeing green shoots pop their heads up out of the ground or through the snow. Those first sprouts from the soil or on a transplant are a welcome sign of life. They testify that things are living, growing, thriving. Those signs don't just occur in springtime, however. It can be just as thrilling, if not more so, to see new growth on our plants during the dog days of summer. Sometimes plants in our garden get so stressed by the intense heat and aridity of our Utah summers that we aren't sure they are going to survive. We have had far too much experience losing plants to the botanical equivalent of heat stroke, and as a result, we worry when we see those signs of stress. One thing, however, eases our fears and assures us that everything will be okay— new growth on the plants. If we don't see new growth, we have real reason to worry. A lack of new growth indicates that the plant is not thriving but is stressed, and if it is not rescued, it will come to a withered, dry demise.

New growth for people, as in plants, is a sign of life. Yet isn't it interesting that many of us shun opportunities for new growth in our lives because of what they might require? New growth always requires a lot of effort and often comes with some degree of personal inconvenience, even discomfort or pain. Stretching ourselves isn't always pleasant, but it always yields a bigger and better self, a more spiritually substantive soul. As Elder Neal A. Maxwell insightfully asked, "If our soul is to be stretched, how can that happen without growing pains?" (*Neal A. Maxwell Quotebook*, 150). In fact, just like plants, we cannot produce the fruit the Lord expects of us if we are not continually growing. That kind of new growth— growth that is soul stretching and pulls us out of our stagnant comfort zones—enables us to experience more fully the abundant life Jesus promised (see John 10:10) and empowers us to bless and serve others with the fruit that will inevitably result from such a life. There are things that we can do to nurture new growth in our lives. Additionally, there are opportunities and experiences that the Lord provides for us when our own efforts are insufficient to produce the requisite and sanctifying soul stretching.

One of the ways we can cultivate new growth in our lives is through continuing to learn

new things. "If the day ever comes when we quit learning, look out," said President Gordon B. Hinckley. "We will just atrophy and die. . . .

"There is great potential within each of us to go on learning. Regardless of our age, unless there be serious illness, we can read, study, drink in the writings of wonderful men and women. . . .

". . . We must go on growing. We must continuously learn. It is a divinely given mandate that we go on adding to our knowledge.

"We have access to institute classes, extension courses, education weeks, and many other opportunities where, as we study and match our minds with others, we will discover a tremendous reservoir of capacity within ourselves" (*Teachings of Gordon B. Hinckley*, 302–3).

New growth from continual learning should be as much a spiritual quest as an intellectual one. Learning affects not just the mind but our entire being. No wonder the Lord, in modern revelation, has admonished us to "seek ye out of the best books words of wisdom" (D&C 88:118) and to "seek ye earnestly the best gifts" (D&C 46:8). As we learn new things and develop new talents, not only are our lives blessed and made more productive but our capacity to bless others is also expanded. The beautification project that comes with new growth—intellectual, spiritual, social, and emotional stretching—affects not only ourselves but in a way the whole community.

Because the "natural man" often resists new growth (Mosiah 3:19), our Father in Heaven provides unexpected opportunities to develop new talents, to cultivate new character traits, and to be drawn out of our shells and comfort zones. These opportunities may come as callings to serve in new and different ways in the Church as well as new (often neither desired nor sought for) challenges in our lives. Examples of new growth opportunities might include such scenarios as the following:

- A gifted musician who has spent years as the ward organist, choir director, or Primary pianist is called to teach the fifteen-year-olds.

- A somewhat reserved man who has served for decades as either a ward or a stake clerk is called to teach the Gospel Doctrine class.

- A grandmother who has served as Relief Society president numerous times is called to be the Beehive advisor in Young Women, though her granddaughters are older than the girls in her class.

- A man who has a lifetime of leadership and teaching experience in the Church and yet can't balance his own checkbook is called to be the ward financial clerk.

- The doting grandparents of a large family (all of whom live within a few blocks) who have never been outside Utah, except on their once-in-a-lifetime pilgrimage to Disneyland, are called to serve as full-time missionaries to Uzbekistan.

No doubt you have had times when you have received callings to positions in the Church that seem totally unlike you, as if the calling came from desperation rather than inspiration or that someone was playing a kind of not-so-funny cosmic prank on you. (For Brent it was being called to be a scoutmaster *for the third time*.)

At other times, an opportunity for new growth may come in the form of difficult and painful circumstances. It may be the death of a loved one, a life-threatening illness, loss of employment and economic security, a bitter divorce, a wayward child, the fading of a lifelong dream, or a myriad of other trials or disappointments. Each can bring out something in us, something that needs to be developed and drawn from our souls and that would not come any other way. The "natural man" will resist, reject, or even rebel against such invitations to stretch and grow (Mosiah 3:19). But if we refuse such invitations, we cease to reach out, our roots shrink, we shut down the processes of growth, and we fade away spiritually.

On the other hand, as devoted disciples who are "alive in Christ" (2 Nephi 25:25), we understand that a lack of new growth—a lack of opportunities to learn new things and develop new skills, a lack of challenges that may stretch us beyond what we think are our limits—means spiritual stagnation and death. We sense that such stretching means that our spiritual roots are sinking deeper into the life-giving soil of the Savior's gospel. Likewise we recognize that new growth stimulates the leaves and branches of our lives to spread wider to catch the enlightening and enlivening rays of His love. His light and life then flows through us, filling us with spiritual vigor, producing sweet and plentiful fruit (see Mosiah 16:9). We will accept the growth opportunity, however inconvenient, illogical, or difficult. Perhaps if we, like a freshly planted seed or an eager transplant, would humbly recognize and accept more opportunities for personal growth, we would be more prepared for difficult challenges and not have to spend so much time learning the hard way. As evidenced in gardens and in God's people, new growth always means life, and eternal growth means eternal life.

TOO MUCH OF A GOOD THING

We lovingly refer to the plants in our yard and garden as our "babies." Often when Brent comes home from work, he will go to the backyard to, as he says, "check on my babies." Gardens are like children in that they require a lot of time, attention, and tender, loving care, and they even need babysitting once in awhile. When we have to go out of town for a few days, arrangements must be made for someone to "watch the babies," meaning, to water the garden. On one occasion, when we were to be gone for several days, our teenage daughter was given that assignment.

"Be sure to water the garden," Brent admonished in a long-distance phone call.

"I'll go do it right now," Janey assured her father.

We were able to relax and enjoy the rest of our vacation knowing that the yard, flowers, and vegetable garden would not be neglected in the unseasonably warm weather. When we returned home, it was a welcome sight to see the grass so green and the flowers blooming as if to greet us with a hearty welcome home. After unloading the luggage from the car, Brent hurriedly went to the backyard to check on his "babies." To his horror, he found the sprinkler was still running full blast, and the vegetable garden looked like Lake Michigan. Not even rice could have grown in that man-made reservoir. There was even more concern and

consternation over whether the vegetable garden could be saved than there was for the sizeable water bill that would inevitably result.

"Oh, I guess I forgot to turn off the water," Janey sheepishly confessed. "You told me to turn on the water. You didn't tell me to turn it off," she rationalized, half-jokingly. Luckily, the garden was in time rehabilitated and yielded a small harvest and a big lesson. We learned that it is possible to have too much of a good thing. It is a lesson that we have had to learn again and again in our lives not only in raising vegetables but also in raising kids.

We have learned that just as there is a delicate balance in nature, so there is need for balance in our own lives and in the lives of our children. When things get out of balance, problems inevitably follow. Those problems may start out small, but they can become large, even catastrophic. Sometimes the problem may be a decline in productivity: we don't become what we were intended to become. For example, we have learned by experience that nitrogen is vital to vigorous and productive plants. That is why we use fertilizer. Too little results in weak and sickly plants. Yet too much can burn the plants and even kill them. We've learned that lesson all too well.

A more common problem we have encountered is that a little too much fertilizer can result in tomato plants that grow vigorously, are a deep, rich, green color, but never produce tomatoes. Flowers, likewise, can be affected when the fertilizer balance is not right. A little too much and instead of beautiful blooms, you get tall, spindly plants that neither "please the eye" nor "gladden the heart" (D&C 59:18). Soil and the nutrients in it, water, and sunshine are absolutely essential to a good garden. However, there must be a proper balance. Too much or too little of any of these imperatives stifles growth and productivity and can, under certain conditions, ultimately kill, no matter how hearty the organism.

People are a lot like plants in this manner. They come in all conditions. Some are hearty, and others are delicate. Some are high maintenance, and others can thrive even under difficult conditions. Yet, for all, a proper balance of life's essential ingredients is crucial for proper growth and productivity. Each of us needs spiritual, social, intellectual, and emotional stimulation. We all need love, affection, and rewarding relationships. We need hard work, self-discipline, and responsibility. Likewise, we need recreation, relaxation, rejuvenation, and even fun. Because we humans are much more complex than potatoes or petunias, we need much more than just sunshine, water, and rich soil. Indeed, it is because of those complex and comprehensive human needs that proper balance in our lives is so critical.

The old adage "All work and no play makes Jack a dull boy" certainly bespeaks a balanced, well-rounded life. There could be numerous variations on that old saying: "All play and no work makes Jack an unproductive (temporally poor and spiritually bankrupt) boy," or "All study and no social life makes Jackie a lonely, withdrawn, straight-A student." You see the point. As Elder M. Russell Ballard said, "Remember, too much of anything in life can throw us off-balance. At the same time, too little of the important things can do the same thing" ("Keeping Life's Demands in Balance," 15).

While Brent presided over a mission a few years ago, we saw up close and personal this need for balance in life with the many missionaries with whom we served. It was not uncommon for a young man or woman to come to the mission field as a high-achieving, disciplined student in school but lacking social skills. Such missionaries were great with books but not so good with people. On the other hand, some missionaries had spent so much time and energy on their social lives that they hadn't made time for scripture study and gaining a solid knowledge of the doctrines they would be teaching as missionaries. Some had played hard but had never held a job and learned the lessons of responsibility, accountability, and hard work that come from that venture. It was not uncommon to hear comments from the elders and sisters that began with the phrase, "I wish had . . ." You can fill in the blank with such phrases as "studied more," "not given up on piano lessons," "paid more attention in seminary," "worked harder," or countless other regrets. Those who hit the ground running and were most prepared to be successful missionaries were those who were balanced—who, like the boy Jesus, had developed spiritually, socially, intellectually, and emotionally (see Luke 2:52).

This principle is just as important to us as parents, church leaders, citizens, and neighbors. If we pay too much attention to one thing—even if that one thing is good—something else, perhaps something even better, will suffer. "As we consider various choices, we should remember that it is not enough that something is good," Elder Dallin H. Oaks declared. "Other choices are better, and still others are best" ("Good, Better, Best," 104–5).

Many gardeners periodically have a scientific soil test done by a horticultural laboratory to determine the balance of the nutrients in the soil. They thus discover that they may have either too much or too little of good things, nutrients that the garden desperately needs. Unfortunately there isn't the same kind of test for people—we can't pack them up and ship them off to a lab hoping to get a detailed description of what needs to be done to make them more productive.

The test we need must be done individually by personal introspection of our priorities, attitudes, actions, and relationships. How is the balance between work and play, spiritual and temporal, social and intellec-tual pursuits? If we don't periodi-cally, carefully, and truthfully test the balance of our lives and make the necessary adjustments, we may never come to know what nutrients are either lacking or are too abun-dant in our lives to yield the fruits that eternally matter. In the scrip-tures the Lord has reminded us that we should not run faster than we have strength. Yet we are to be dili-

gent and do things in their proper order (see Mosiah 4:27; D&C 10:4). The phrase "proper order" means more than sequence; it involves the proper balance of things as well as proper priorities. "Moderation in all things" is another phrase we often use. Perhaps it could be better said, "Balance in all things." Obtaining that crucial balance is, as Elder Neal A. Maxwell said, "one of the keenest tests of our agency." He elaborated: "So often our hardest choices are between competing and desirable alternatives (each with righteous consequences), when there is not time to do both at once. Indeed, it is at these mortal intersections—where time and talent and opportunities meet—that priorities, like traffic lights, are sorely needed" (*Notwithstanding My Weakness*, 5).

It takes a vigilant gardener to ensure that a garden's soil has the proper balance of nutrients. It takes a vigilant disciple to be continually more watchful of a soul's condition—one's spirituality and family relationships—than of tulips and tomatoes; to be more aware of the balance (or lack of it) in our lives than we are of the pH factor of our garden soil.

There is another aspect to this important lesson we have learned about the dangers of too much of a good thing. We learned it by trying to establish a healthy lawn. When grass is first planted, it needs to be kept moist. Too much water, however, will flood the area, resulting in either drowning the seeds so they do not sprout or washing the seeds away from where we want the lush grass, leaving some patches where there is no grass and others where there is more grass than we want. To help the lawn become firmly established, we have to cut back on the water. It may seem to defy logic, but if the grass is pampered by being watered too frequently, it will not establish a deep root system. Plants certainly need water, but they need roots that are deep enough to support them and provide necessary sustenance.

We are like that as well. We need deep roots more than we need lush foliage. Heavenly Father knows that better than anyone. As a result, He knows that pampering—a life without real challenges, hardships, and heartaches, a life with too much of a good thing—does not promote significant spiritual growth and leaves the person with shallow roots. Lacking deep roots of character, one is easily weighed down, broken off, or blown away. The Savior provides us with the ultimate root system. C. S. Lewis observed:

"God, who has made us, knows what we are and that our happiness lies in Him. Yet we will not seek it in Him as long as He leaves us any other resort where it can even plausibly be looked for. While what we call 'our own life' remains agreeable we will not surrender it to Him. What then can God do in our interests but make 'our own life' less agreeable to us, and take away the plausible sources of false happiness? It is just here, where God's providence seems at first to be most cruel, that the Divine humility, the stooping down of the Highest, most deserves praise" (*Problem of Pain*, 85–86).

Too much of a good thing, whether it be in our own spiritual development or in our attempts to rear a righteous family, usually ends up being a bad thing. Often less is more. Maintaining a proper balance in life is important. Having deep spiritual roots is essential. Trusting in God and His purposes for us—even when it is uncomfortable—is imperative.

PERENNIALS

We are particularly fond of perennials, though not because they are the most beautiful plants that produce the most spectacular blooms, because often they aren't and they don't. There are annuals that are far more showy. But perennials are like their category name declares: perennial. The word is defined as "present at all seasons of the year" and "persisting for several years" (*Merriam-Webster's 11th,* s.v. "perennial"). Translated into Utah Valley garden-ese, *perennial* means plants that just keep coming back year after year and don't need a lot of extra care—low maintenance, high yield. And that is a valuable gospel lesson we have learned in the garden. We want to be perennial, or, like the word's synonyms, *persistent, enduring, constant,* and *perpetual.*

To those who believed on His words, Jesus declared, "If ye *continue* in my word, *then* are ye my disciples indeed" (John 8:31; emphasis added). It was not mere belief that determined discipleship. It was persistence—continuing to believe, to do, to love, to serve, to obey as Christ had taught and exemplified. The Apostle Paul admonished the young disciple Timothy to "*continue* thou in the things which thou hast learned and hast been assured of" (2 Timothy 3:14; emphasis added). Likewise, Paul taught the Colossian Saints to "*continue* in the faith grounded and settled" and not be "moved away from the hope

of the gospel" (Colossians 1:23). In similar language, the Book of Mormon describes perennial disciples as "steadfast and immovable in keeping the commandments of God" (Alma 1:25). Constancy, consistency, and continuing—"press[ing] forward with a steadfastness in Christ" (2 Nephi 31:20)—are hallmark characteristics of a perennial disciple. "Quiet, sustained goodness is the order of heaven," Elder Neal A. Maxwell stated, "not conspicuous or episodic busyness" (*Notwithstanding My Weakness*, 5). In Lehi's vision of the tree of life we see that those who continued to hold fast to the iron rod and persistently pressed forward ultimately partook of the delicious fruit of eternal life, a fruit that "was desirable above all other fruit" and filled the soul "with exceedingly great joy" (1 Nephi 8:12). Those who were not constant, who failed to continue, and who let go of the rod were lost in the "mist of darkness," drowned in the "depths of the fountain," or defected to the great and spacious building (1 Nephi 8:23, 32). A perennial disciple hangs on when others give up.

William Wilson Sterrett, a nineteenth-century

convert to the Church, exemplifies what it means to be a perennial, rather than seasonal, disciple. Full of gold fever and a spirit of adventure, young William arrived in Salt Lake City on his way to seek his fortune in the goldfields of California. "During the winter of 1850," William recorded, "I read the *Book of Mormon, Voice of Warning,* and some other works, and I became convinced of the truth. The Holy Ghost enlightened my mind to the extent that I knew for myself of the truth, that it was of God." Sterrett explained that many Gentiles wintered over in Salt Lake City before venturing on to California. Many of these Gentiles, having a desire to fit in and benefit from the hospitality of the Saints, joined the Church during the winter. They were known as "Winter Mormons," for in the spring they bade farewell not only to Salt Lake City but also to their professed beliefs in Mormonism. Despite a burning testimony, William Sterrett purposely delayed his baptism until early May. "I held off," he recalled, "not wishing to be called a 'Winter Mormon'" (in *Voices from the Past,* 53–54). Because he was truly converted and consecrated to the Lord, William Sterrett, unlike the "Winter Mormons" of his day, continued to keep his covenants, serve his God, and live the gospel he had embraced.

Today there are likewise seasonal saints who may take upon themselves the covenants and commitments of the gospel. They may be active for a season but do not press forward, persevering and producing continually. There are perhaps as many reasons for this as there are varieties of flowers in our gardens. Whatever the reason, however, the result is the same: faith that withers, spiritual roots that cannot sustain the soul, obedience to the Lord's commandments and service in His kingdom that fade and fall away. If we are not perennial in our faithful discipleship—"steadfast and immovable" (Mosiah 5:15)—in keeping our covenants, we die spiritually. The scriptures repeatedly speak of enduring to the end, as well. Enduring in faith is really nothing more than being perennial, persistent, perpetual. "Even yesterday's spiritual experience does not guarantee us against tomorrow's relapse," wrote Elder Neal A. Maxwell. "Persistence thus matters greatly" (*If Thou Endure It Well*, 122).

Even for perennial plants there are seasons, however, seasons when growth is dramatic, seasons when blooms may be profuse, and seasons of dormancy. But when perennials are dormant they are still alive and storing energy for the next season of growth. In our own lives, there is "a season, and a time to every purpose" (Ecclesiastes 3:1), times when we are more active or productive than at other times, times when circumstances may even necessitate a season of relative dormancy. Yet in all of these seasons, we are truly perennial disciples if we remain constant in our love for the Lord, seek continually to feed our souls, strengthen our testimony, and serve in whatever way our circumstances permit.

We love perennials because they keep coming back and keep producing. In fact, the more we garden, the more we depend on perennials. They are so reliable, consistent, and constant, continuing to provide beauty to our yard year after year, season after season, with relatively little maintenance. We want to be perennials in God's garden, disciples who are tried and true, disciples who do their job and don't complain, who don't require constant propping up or special handling, who continue to "press forward with a steadfastness in Christ," even after years and years of faithful service (2 Nephi 31:20). God be thanked for perennials in His kingdom!

PATIENCE AND IMPATIENS

Strolling through a nursery one day admiring the vast array of beautiful blooms and shrubs and trees of every kind, Brent was stopped in his tracks as he read the label on a pony-pack of bedding plants. "Impatience?" he teased. "Why do they sell impatience? Gardeners have plenty of that. We need patience. Why don't they sell that?" To which Wendy responded, "Impatiens—I-M-P-A-T-I-E-N-S; not impatience—I-M-P-A-T-I-E-N-C-E." Every year as we plant impatiens in our gardens, we think of that conversation and remember the need to be patient not only with our impatiens and other plants but also with ourselves, our lives, our circumstances, and our spiritual progress. Impatience is one of the chief characteristics of the natural man, and that is why it comes so naturally. In contrast, patience—or longsuffering, as the scriptures often call it—is an essential attribute of godliness, an attribute that requires cultivation and yes, patience.

Patience is one of the most important lessons a gardener learns, albeit not always willingly or cheerfully. It takes patience to wait for seeds to germinate, to grow, to produce blooms, or bear fruit or vegetables. It takes patience to wait for the snow to melt so that we can work in our garden. Impatience never speeds up the process of warming the soil or germinating seeds. Impatience never bears fruit, either in our gardens or in our souls. Someone once cleverly quipped, "Patience is the art of hiding our impatience." Gardening allows us to do just that.

Striving for perfection is like striving to have a bounteous harvest from our garden—it takes time and effort. Neither perfection nor sweet corn comes quickly. As President Dieter F. Uchtdorf taught, walking the path of discipleship requires walking in patience. "Too often we approach the gospel like a farmer who places a seed in the ground in the morning and expects corn on the cob by the afternoon. When Alma compared the word of God to a seed, he explained that the seed grows into a fruit-bearing tree gradually, as a result of our 'faith, and [our] diligence, and patience, and long-suffering'" (Uchtdorf, "We Are Doing a Great Work," 75).

The scriptures often speak of patience in the context of trust—trust in God, His ways, His purposes for us, and His timetable. "Rest in the Lord, and wait patiently for him," the psalmist wrote (Psalm 37:7).

"Patience is tied very closely to faith in our Heavenly Father," stated Elder Neal A. Maxwell. "Actually, when we are unduly impatient we are suggesting that we know what is best—better than does God. Or, at least, we are asserting that our timetable is better than His. Either way we are questioning the reality of God's omniscience as if, as some seem to believe, God were on some sort of postdoctoral fellowship and were not quite in charge of everything. . . .

"When we are impatient, we are neither reverential nor reflective because we are too self-centered. Whereas faith and patience are companions, so are selfishness and impatience. . . .

"Clearly, without patience we will learn less in life. We will see less; we will feel less; we will hear less. Ironically, 'rush' and 'more' usually mean 'less.' The pressure of 'now,' time and time again, goes against the grain of the gospel with its eternalism.

"There is also in patience a greater opportunity for that discernment which sorts out the things that matter most from the things that matter least" ("Patience," 215–18).

Perhaps nothing tries our patience more than personal trials and tribulations. But that is the way it is supposed to be, an integral part of the plan of salvation and the purpose of life. The Apostle Paul taught that "tribulation worketh patience" (Romans 5:3). We came to earth to gain experience and to obtain an education that will prepare us for exaltation. That education is often found in the school of hard knocks. Elder Orson F. Whitney taught: "No pain that we suffer, no trial that we experience is wasted. It ministers to our education, to the development of such qualities as patience, faith, fortitude and humility." And

if we endure it patiently and learn the lessons God is teaching, it "builds up our characters, purifies our hearts, expands our souls, and makes us more tender and charitable, more worthy to be called the children of God" (quoted in Kimball, *Faith Precedes the Miracle*, 98).

About mid-July, when the corn is four or five feet tall and green tomatoes are on the vine, we get really impatient for things to ripen. Oh, how we want sweet corn on the cob and vine-ripened tomatoes right then and there. We can almost taste them. But it is not time yet. We can be frustrated, or we can be patient. We can either continue to weed and water and wait, or we can angrily pull up the tomato vines and cut down the corn stalks. One is hard and slow; the other is quick and easy. One leads in due time to the very sweetness we long desired, and the other leaves us empty and unfilled. So it is with our lives. No wonder the Lord often reminds us to bear our adversities and afflictions with patience (see Alma 26:27). He wants us to taste the fruit of the love of God, the fruit that is sweeter and more delicious than anything else. But it will never be obtained if we impatiently give up and give in when the heat is on.

Lastly, gardening has taught us that we must be as patient with ourselves and those around us as we are with our plants. Do we, as Elder Neal A. Maxwell once said, "[pull] up the daisies to see how the roots are doing?" (*Neal A. Maxwell Quotebook*, 13). Or do we cut down a tree because it is only ten feet tall instead of eleven? Of course not! Similarly, we must not browbeat ourselves or mercilessly drive others with unrealistic expectations. Brent's mother had a plaque on her kitchen wall that said, "God grant me patience—right now!" All too often we are like that. We can replace the word *patience* with any number of other desired attributes. "God grant me gospel knowledge—right now!" "God grant me personal righteousness—right now! Or "God grant me increased spirituality—right now!" It doesn't work like that. Attributes of godliness and character are developed and refined over time. One of the best ways that we can cultivate patience is to more keenly observe and appreciate progress and direction rather than obsess about how far away we are from our eternal destination. Like gardeners, we do all we can—we plant the seeds, nourish the plants, eliminate the weeds—and then wait upon the Lord. "Wait on the Lord: be of good courage, and he shall strengthen thine heart: wait, I say, on the Lord" (Psalm 27:14). Waiting on the Lord, the Christlike attribute of patience, implies active submission to His will and His ultimate designs for our lives. It is not about our plans and schedules. It is about His will and His way. When we remember that and practice it, patience always leads to perfection (see D&C 67:13).

THE ABUNDANT HARVEST

He who plants a garden works hand in hand with God." If you are a passionate gardener, you have probably felt spiritual stirrings as you have knelt upon the moist ground molding rich brown earth with your hands. Or perhaps you have had intimations of the joy of creation as you stood back to survey the fruits of your horticultural efforts and pronounced them good. There is nothing on earth that stirs in gardeners a sense of having riches and abundance like a yard full of flowers, fruits, and vegetables. Being able to walk out your back door and pluck a homegrown tomato and a fresh cucumber from the garden to add to your dinner or to snip some basil and parsley from a pot to make your own flavorings and garnishes or to pick and snack on a sweet, sun-warmed strawberry as you mow the lawn is as good as living in the Garden of Eden, as far as we're concerned. One could feel like Adam or Eve while gathering a kaleidoscope of blooms from generous flower beds to arrange in a vase on the kitchen table. Catching the fragrance of lilacs or lilies on the breeze in your own backyard is a fleeting glimpse of paradisiacal glory. It seems like the whole world is yours when surrounded by such temporal and spiritual profusion. Whether you live in a desert or on a tropical island, on a lush expansive acreage or in an apartment with a few plants in pots on the patio, when you are harvesting the fruits of your own devoted labors, it doesn't matter—you feel the Love.

The Love is Heavenly Father and His Son, Jesus Christ, the creator of this fallen yet amply provisioned world. Every particle of this earth bespeaks His perfect love and concern:

"He that ascended up on high, as also he descended below all things, in that he comprehended all things, that he might be in all and through all things, the light of truth;

"Which truth shineth. This is the light of Christ. As also he is in the sun, and the light of the sun, and the power thereof by which it was made.

"As also he is in the moon, and is the light of the moon, and the power thereof by which it was made;

"As also the light of the stars, and the power thereof by which they were made;

"And the earth also, and the power thereof, even the earth upon which you stand.

"And the light which shineth, which giveth you light, is through him who enlighteneth your eyes, which is the same light that quickeneth your understandings;

"Which light proceedeth forth from the presence of God to fill the immensity of space—

"The light which is in all things, which giveth life to all things, which is the law by which all things are governed, even the power of God who sitteth upon his throne, who is in the bosom of eternity, who is in the midst of all things" (D&C 88:6–13).

Accordingly, every miraculous flower is a glimpse of His beauty and hints of the delights beyond this life He has prepared for us. Each marvelous fruit bears testimony of the eternal and infinite abundance we will one day find in His presence. Trees and grasses that coat the earth seem to symbolize the hope for a better life made possible by Him. Even the most barren stretches of earth are teeming with life in some form, witnessing that everything He creates is good and life-affirming. All things are made to testify of Him. All things bear record of Him. Why? Because they are the logical, inevitable, earthly unfolding of and expression of Him. They could not be otherwise: They are evidences, clues, manifestations, and telltale signs of His personal presence, His truths, and His loving-kindness and care for each of us. He thoughtfully engineered for us—for each individual—infinitely detailed beauties and stunningly captivating vistas "both to please the eye and to gladden the heart; yea, for food and for raiment, for taste and for smell, to strengthen the body and to enliven the soul" (D&C 59:18–19). He wanted us to feel enriched, encircled, and infused with His love and

His Spirit. A longtime favorite Primary song first awakened us to an awareness of the love expressed in His creation.

> Whenever I hear the song of a bird
> Or look at the blue, blue sky,
> Whenever I feel the rain on my face
> Or the wind as it rushes by,
>
> Whenever I touch a velvet rose
> Or walk by our lilac tree,
> I'm glad that I live in this beautiful world
> Heav'nly Father created for me.
>
> He gave me my eyes that I might see
> The color of butterfly wings.
> He gave me my ears that I might hear
> The magical sound of things.
> He gave me my life, my mind, my heart:
> I thank him rev'rently
> For all his creations, of which I'm a part.
> Yes, I know Heav'nly Father loves me.

("My Heavenly Father Loves Me," *Children's Songbook*, 228–29)

Like the abundance of His love, as manifest in His wondrous plan of salvation and His miraculous Atonement, "the earth is full, and there is enough and to spare" (D&C 104:17). And though the earth may be temporary and subject to natural disasters that cause suffering and starvation, there will never be a famine or a drought or a scarcity of His love. To think that we have the opportunity to be loved like this, to take part in this great merciful plan of love! If we had no other blessing, it would be enough just to have been given the chance to be here, and yet, it is only a harbinger, a likeness of what will one day be a fulness, a harvest of eternal abundance beyond our current ability to comprehend (see Maxwell, "In Him All Things Hold Together," 8).

THE TREE OF LIFE

We had a peach tree in our backyard that grew big, beautiful, sweet, juicy peaches. One spring Mother Nature heavily thinned our peach blossoms with her long frosty fingers. By harvest time there were a few mediocre fruits and one plump lonely peach that hung all by itself on a branch at the very top of the tree. Wendy watched with mouth-watering anticipation as the large peach ripened slowly, tantalizingly in the late summer sun. It beckoned to her as no other peach had ever done before. She waited patiently for just the right day and hour to relieve the tree of its loftiest, most portly peach.

When the auspicious day finally arrived, Wendy carefully climbed the tree and gingerly retrieved her prize. On her way down, she lost her footing. The next thing she knew she was skydiving without a parachute or safety net and landed flat on the ground. She received several scrapes and a deep bruise from the concrete curbing she landed on. Worse, her beloved peach was half-crushed in her hand and covered in soil and mulch. She was badly shaken, but all she could think about was consuming the now juicier but damaged peach before the flavor could degrade or leak out. Despite the pain, she jumped quickly to her feet, ran directly into the house, rinsed the peach under the kitchen faucet, and then savored each sloppy bite. As she took the last bite of this extraordinarily sweet peach, she determined that it was worth the wait, the unladylike topple from the tree, the painful and colorful bruise from knee to hip.

We have joked many times since that day about how badly Wendy wanted that fruit. Though comical, it sometimes brings to mind the more serious metaphor of Lehi's vision of the difficult quest to obtain the miraculous fruit of the tree of life. It also evokes the words of an old song that has become a favorite Christmas carol of ours, entitled "Jesus Christ the Apple Tree":

> *The Tree of Life my soul hath seen*
> *Laden with fruit and always green.*
> *The trees of nature fruitless be*
> *Compared to Christ the apple tree.*
>
> (Author unknown)

Centuries ago, when this verse was written, the word *apple* meant any round fruit.

The tree of life was commonly seen as a symbol for Jesus Christ among Christians, and it served from ancient times as the symbol of a god in many other religions. Christ, our Creator, lovingly crafted trees, especially fruit trees, to bear testimony of Him and teach us about His life, His powers, His attributes, and His plan for our salvation. Every tree around us can be a powerful visual reminder of Him and the joyous blessings He offers us.

In the scriptures, we are first introduced to the tree of life in the Garden of Eden. Adam and Eve are free to partake of it until they become mortal by partaking of the fruit of another important and symbolic tree, the tree of knowledge of good and evil. After they are driven from the garden and have posterity, Adam and Eve teach their children about the two trees. Through precept, example, and temple symbolism, they learn that they must choose the good instead of the evil in order to return to the tree of life. Its unexcelled fruit, we learn from the Book of Mormon, is "most precious, . . . sweet above all that is sweet, . . . white above all that is white, yea, and pure above all that is pure" (Alma 32:42). It is the eternal love and life of God as manifested in the holy atoning sacrifice of His Only Begotten Son. It is Jesus Christ Himself.

Though many of Adam and Eve's posterity lost sight of the tree of life as Jesus Christ, they borrowed the symbol of the tree as a representative of their own gods. They remembered bits and pieces of the story of salvation and developed their own versions of the narrative. Though the story was changed from culture to culture and down through the centuries, recognizable themes have endured. The rich stories and legends surrounding the symbolic tree of life can bring us new perspective about the universal love and mission of Christ.

The tree of life symbolically unites and holds three worlds in its power—hell, earth, and heaven. Its roots reach deep to lay the foundations of the earth. The tree usually grows near a beautiful stream or fountain, where its roots also bring restraint and order to the unruly waters of the underworld beneath. When the water emerges from the roots of the tree, it is a life-giving force to all it touches (see 1 Nephi 11:25). Further, the towering branches of the tree represent the great expanse of heaven. They protect and uphold all living things, while also providing shade and shelter to those who seek refuge below. The tree is often considered the symbol of a temple or the abode of the gods, as well.

As with Christ, the magnificent tree also symbolizes crucifixion and resurrection in many traditions. Crucifixion was originally performed on a tree. Criminals or enemies were lifted up and hanged on or nailed to a tree to humiliate them and display their misfortune as a warning to others. The Apostle Paul refers to Jesus being hanged on a tree and being made a curse to take away our curse (see Galatians 3:13). The crosses of Christ's day were simply hand-hewn substitutes for a tree.

On the other hand, the miraculous return of life in the spring to a seemingly dead and barren tree also makes it a powerful symbol of resurrection. Christianity is not the only tradition in which the tree or a cross represents a god who, according to belief, was crucified and resurrected. Some believe the decorated Christmas tree originated as a symbol honoring Attis, the crucified god of the Greeks, and was later adopted as a symbol of Christ by Christians.

In further symbolism that Latter-day Saints can appreciate, the tree of life is not easily obtained. The journey to find it is difficult and dangerous, especially because of some kind of evil creature or god who jealously guards its roots and in at least one case, gnaws at them. We know from the account in Genesis that "cherubims and a flaming sword" were assigned to keep Adam and Eve from partaking of the fruit of the tree of life in their fallen mortal state (Genesis 3:24). The road back to it would be long and lead through toil, temptation, tribulation, and the Atonement of Jesus Christ.

The fruit of the tree has perhaps the richest symbolism of all, and its full meaning is understood only through the restored gospel. We learn from the

Book of Mormon that the fruit is the most beautiful to the eye, the sweetest to the taste, and the purest to the soul of any other fruit. It is to be desired above all things. The flesh of the fruit may represent the Word made flesh on earth and, figuratively, in man (see John 1:14). As one partakes of it continually, it diffuses throughout the spirit and body and becomes one with the being of the partaker. As this process proceeds, we crucify the old man of sin and are resurrected to new life in Christ. "As the tree grows inside one's soul, the image of Christ begins to appear in one's countenance. Through a person's faith in Christ, one receives additional gifts of the Holy Spirit made possible by the Atonement and becomes a partaker of the divine nature. He puts off the natural man and becomes Christlike. One is born again by the power of the Atonement and the Holy Spirit" (Bateman, "Lehi's Tree and Alma's Seed," 31).

There are many, perhaps countless, other lessons to be learned from the tree of life, but one of the most important is the symbol of its seeds as a symbol of eternal life. The tree perpetuates itself through the seeds in its fruit. Hence, the "continuation of the seeds" represents not only eternal life through the Atonement of the Son of God but also eternal posterity (D&C 132:19).

These are but a few thoughts on the beauty and meaning of the tree of life that have amazed and enriched us. There is so much more to be discovered by study, meditation, and revelation. The next time you see and admire the beauty and usefulness of a tree, we invite you to contemplate what Christ is teaching you personally through this instructive creation that bears singular witness of Him. The next time you eat an apple, whether from your own home orchard or from the store, think of Christ, His perfect life, His perfect love, and His infinite Atonement.

His beauty doth all things excel:
By faith I know, but ne'er can tell,
The glory which I now can see
In Jesus Christ the apple tree.

For happiness I long have sought,
And pleasure dearly I have bought:
I missed of all; but now I see
'Tis found in Christ the apple tree.

I'm weary with my former toil,
Here I will sit and rest a while:
Under the shadow I will be,
Of Jesus Christ the apple tree.

This fruit doth make my soul to thrive,
It keeps my dying faith alive:
Which makes my soul in haste to be
With Jesus Christ the apple tree.

(Author unknown)

THE BEST-LAID PLANTS

In the spring, our neighbors often find us in our yard standing and staring intently at the same piece of ground for long periods of time. It needs to be planted with something, but what? What will grow there? What accents are needed? What do we love? What will our color scheme be for this summer? How would the new plant we saw at the garden shop fit in this space? After hours of thinking, planning, and checking labels and prices, we have created a landscape in our minds that rivals a Thomas Kinkade painting. Likewise, when we have mentally dedicated portions of our garden to various vegetables, we picture a neat, weed-free, thriving green patch of perfectly straight rows lined up like disciplined soldiers in formation. And then we set out to make our vision a reality. What a great joy it is to plant everything you want in just the place you want it with just the results you planned!

It's too bad that doesn't always happen in this life, either with plants or with people. The promise of perfection is for the next life. On this earth, "life is what happens when you are making other plans," as someone has said. We may start out with the best of intentions and the most carefully laid plans, but the mortal whose life goes exactly as scripted is most likely nonexistent. Likewise, with gardening, even if you can find just the right plant for the right spot, it may not grow exactly the way you envisioned it. Each plant has

its own DNA and its own potential for variety. Furthermore, it may get a disease, the soil may not be optimal, or the sprinkler system may not be adjusted adequately for it. Seeds that are painstakingly planted, even with the use of instruments to create straight rows, can be moved out of place by rain or birds or wind or weeds or even grandchildren. Seeds can fail to sprout or crowd each other or grow in the wrong direction. As for weeds, keeping a garden weed-free is relatively easy at first but then requires increasingly greater effort and enthusiasm as more weeds invade, the weather gets hot, and other things demand your attention. And if a plant does grow perfectly, bugs may damage it, or someone may step on it and smash it.

In other words, life, like any growing thing, takes its own unexpected path, depending on the course God has decreed for it and the endless, seemingly random possibilities that may alter or influence it in this world. Knowing this as we do, it is a wonder that we still spend so much effort and emotion trying to be in total control of outcomes. We still create unrealistic expectations and mental pictures of how things are supposed to be that cause us unnecessary pain and disillusionment when they are not realized. We paint landscapes in our minds of what future success and happiness will look like, and then we become slaves to those pictures, however incorrect or unrealistic they may be. These pictures often extend to others, such as our spouse and children, over whose course we have no control. When we try to force our lives and others' to conform to the naïve pictures in our heads, we are preventing the Lord from planting us in His perfect and eternal landscape. Our yard and garden, as summer wears on, are never as beautiful in reality as in our impossible dreams, especially when the high desert heat of Utah summers is unusually relentless.

Nevertheless, every living thing is a miraculous gift to be relished. And there are moments of sheer bliss when breathtaking flowers bloom and generous trees give cooling shade and hedges are neatly trimmed and the air smells of freshly mowed grass. There is joy at the first produce from the garden and in sharing it with neighbors and preserving it for an uncertain future. And in the end, the weeds and imperfections that seemed to be taking over in August are dead and forgotten with the first frost in October.

So it is with life and its imperfections. Our marriages, through countless adjustments and adaptations, turn out far different from what we expected, but if we hang on and let the Lord be the Master Gardener, they can be much more rewarding and productive than anything we could design. Our children do not always grow according to our landscape blueprints but emerge according to their own inner pattern and the outward circumstances and challenges they must endure. Like some of the plants we trustingly purchase at the nursery, our own lives may turn out to be a completely different plant from what the label promised. And yet, when we plant and sow the best we can and learn to let the harvest be the Lord's, we will be richly satisfied and lack for nothing of worth. It may not come out the way we pictured it, but it will be lovingly fitted to us. Then, in the end, when the wintry hand of death touches our corruptible lives and takes us home, the weeds and weaknesses of this mortal world will be forgotten. Our Savior will prepare us for perfection and plant us in the eternal garden of His Father. There we will find that we are living in a landscape beyond our sweetest dreams.

Thou who knowest all our weakness,
Leave us not to sow alone!
Bid thine angels guard the furrows
Where the precious grain is sown,
Till the fields are crowned with glory,
Filled with mellow, ripened ears,
Filled with fruit of life eternal
From the seed we sowed in tears.

("We Are Sowing," *Hymns*, no. 216)

THE PROMISE OF SPRING

Winter is difficult for gardeners—at least it is for us. It often seems like we are in a holding pattern, waiting for the first signs of spring so that we can get to work in the yard and sink our hands into the soil. Of course, there are things that can be done during the cold and snowy months, but usually we spend our time poring over seed catalogs, planning out what we will be planting in our flower beds and garden plot, and then waiting. It is difficult to wait when we are notoriously impatient.

Spring fever is for gardeners like Christmas anticipation is for young children. When our son was young, he would be almost sick with excitement for Christmas. He would spend hours longingly looking at the toy catalog, putting together his wish list, and counting the days until Santa came. We now know where he got it—Brent does the same thing with seed catalogs! We can be like a child in a toy store when the local nurseries get their new spring stock of seeds and bedding plants. Just as children will excitedly look out the windows on Christmas Eve in hopes of catching a glimpse of Saint Nick and his reindeer, so too will avid adult gardeners longingly gaze out the same windows, waiting for the snow to melt and for the first sign of a crocus or a daffodil poking its head out of the ground. Yes, waiting for spring is difficult. Some years the wait is longer than others, but spring inevitably arrives. It

is this absolute assurance that spring will indeed arrive—no matter how difficult or prolonged the winter has been, or whether the groundhog sees his shadow or not—that gives hope and encouragement when temperatures are most frigid, the snow deepest, and the north wind most biting.

The cold and dreariness of winter always gives way to the warmth and color of spring. The earth that in many aspects seems so lifeless in the dead of winter comes back to life in spring. This yearly transformation, this regeneration of life, is miraculous and truly awesome to behold. The newness of life we see in nature each spring is but a type and shadow of the newness of life that comes to man by reason of Christ's atoning sacrifice. The promise of spring portends the promise of Easter—light and life, resurrection and renewal.

Our mothers both passed away during the winter—Brent's mother on a dreary day in January, and Wendy's on Christmas night. While it is never easy to lose a parent, a child, or any loved one, the loss seems extra painful as you stand ankle-deep (or deeper) in snow looking down on the grave as the harsh wind threatens to freeze your tears to your face. If there was neither the promise of spring nor the hope of life after death, we would be, as the Apostle Paul declared, "of all men most miserable" (1 Corinthians 15:19). Just as spring always follows winter, death will inevitably be swallowed up by life, immortality and eternal life made possible by the death and resurrection of the Lord Jesus Christ. Just as spring flowers break forth from the earth, someday our mothers and fathers, brothers and sisters, sons and daughters, and all mankind will break forth from their graves in glorious resurrection. That promise is sure!

"Now, there is a death which is called a temporal death; and the death of Christ shall loose the bands of this temporal death, that all shall be raised from this temporal death.

"The spirit and the body shall be reunited again in its perfect form; both limb and joint shall be restored to its proper frame, even as we now are at this time; and we shall

be brought to stand before God, knowing even as we know now, and have a bright recollection of all our guilt.

"Now, this restoration shall come to all, both old and young, both bond and free, both male and female, both the wicked and the righteous; and even there shall not so much as a hair of their heads be lost; but every thing shall be restored to its perfect frame, as it is now, or in the body. . . .

"Now, behold, I have spoken unto you concerning the death of the mortal body, and also concerning the resurrection of the mortal body. I say unto you that this mortal body is raised to an immortal body, that is from death, even from the first death unto life, that they can die no more; their spirits uniting with their bodies, never to be divided; thus the whole becoming spiritual and immortal, that they can no more see corruption" (Alma 11:42–45).

We gained a greater appreciation for the way spring symbolizes the Resurrection while we were living in the Midwest as Brent presided over the Illinois Peoria Mission. We observed gardening on a much grander scale than we had attempted in our little yard and garden plot in Utah Valley suburbia. We both had grown up in southeastern Idaho and thought we had seen farmland, but that was nothing like the farms of America's heartland. All around us for miles and miles and miles (and that is not an exaggeration) were fields of corn and soybeans. We arrived in Illinois in midsummer when the fields were a rich, deep green and the corn was tall. In the fall when the fields turned golden brown, the corn and beans were harvested by the ton. It was an amazing sight to watch.

In the winter months after the harvest, not only is the weather drab and dismal but what stubble remains in the fields is lifeless and colorless. In fact, it can be depressing when there is nothing but gray, flat, empty fields as far as the eye can see. Only a blanket of freshly fallen snow or glistening icicles on leftover cornstalks after an ice storm break the monotony of the drabness. No wonder we talk about the winter blahs.

Then, just when it seems we can't bear another day of winter, the whole world slowly begins to come to life. Fields that seemed lonely and abandoned are soon abuzz with activity—tractors

tilling and fertilizing the soil and planting, the first signs of spring in America's bread-basket. The lifeless fields of winter are miraculously transformed in short order. The freshly plowed and planted fields revive, rich brown soil is exposed, seeds are planted, and soon a vibrant green color is seen for miles around. The death that comes with winter is swallowed up by the newness of life that accompanies spring, for death and decomposition are only temporary and preparatory. The promise of spring testifies of the greater light and life that always follow the cold, dreariness, and seeming lifelessness of winter. President Gordon B. Hinckley captured this truth in a poem he wrote while attending the funeral of a friend. The poem was later put to music by Janice Kapp Perry and sung at President Hinckley's funeral by the Mormon Tabernacle Choir.

What is this thing that men call death,
This quiet passing in the night?
'Tis not the end, but genesis
Of better worlds and greater light.

O God, touch Thou my aching heart,
And calm my troubled, haunting fears.
Let hope and faith, transcendent, pure,
Give strength and peace beyond my tears.

There is no death, but only change
With recompense for victory won;

The gift of Him who loved all men,
The Son of God, the Holy One.
("The Empty Tomb Bore Testimony,"
Ensign, May 1988, 66)

The Atonement of Jesus Christ extends to us a promise of spring that goes beyond the promised glorious resurrection from the dead. Some suffer long periods of spiritual winter filled with sicknesses and sorrows. Sometimes there are seasons, long or short, of emotional cold and dreariness, of heartaches, disappointments, and loneliness. Some may feel at times that the field of their lives is empty, barren, unproductive. When in the darkness of despair, depression, and doubt, some feel that the seeds of faith they planted long ago will never germinate and produce fruit, as Alma promised (see Alma 32). To all of these, the Lord's promise of spring is one of hope—hope for "better worlds and greater light" now, not just in the next life. His empty tomb holds out promise to us of our own graves someday being emptied, but also a promise of succor and strength *here and now,* not just a resurrected body *then and there.* The remarkable transformation

of the earth in springtime testifies that no matter how deep the snow and how cold and dreary the winter, there will yet be more warmth, greater sunlight, and a bounteous harvest—warmth and light and life promised by *the* Light and Life of the world. "He will take upon him their infirmities, that his bowels may be filled with mercy, according to the flesh," Alma prophesied, "that he may know according to the flesh how to succor his people according to their infirmities" (Alma 7:12).

Elder Neal A. Maxwell declared: "Can we, even in the depths of disease, tell Him anything at all about suffering? In ways we cannot comprehend, our sicknesses and infirmities were borne by Him even before they were borne by us. The very weight of our combined sins caused Him to descend below all. We have never been, nor will we be, in depths such as He has known. Thus His Atonement made perfect His empathy and His mercy and His capacity to succor us, for which we can be everlastingly grateful as He tutors us in our trials. There was no ram in the thicket at Calvary to spare Him, this Friend of Abraham" (*Neal A. Maxwell Quote Book*, 23).

Because of our knowledge of the Atonement, acquired both by study and by personal experience, we cannot look upon the advent of springtime as a merely temporal occurrence. Trees that seemed lifeless in winter burst with buds and blossoms in spring. A lawn that was brown and, by all appearances, dead, miraculously becomes green again. Springtime is filled with many such miracles. As we see them unfold, we think of Christ and feel overpowering gratitude to Him. Each bud and bloom is a symbol of Him, His sacrifice, His tender mercies, His goodness, and His promises. Surely, along with the promise of spring, as Nephi declared, "all things which have been given of God from the beginning of the world, unto man, are the typifying of him" (2 Nephi 11:4). Every seed planted, every flower that blooms, every vegetable we harvest, and every shrub and tree—in fact, everything in our gardens—testifies of Him and teaches us of His gospel.

WORKS CITED

Atwater, P. M. H. *Coming Back to Life*. New York: Dodd, Mead, and Co., 1988.

Ball, Terry B., and Nathan Winn. *Making Sense of Isaiah: Insights and Modern Applications*. Salt Lake City: Deseret Book, 2009.

Ballard, M. Russell. "Keeping Life's Demands in Balance." *Ensign*, May 1987, 13–16.

Bateman, Merrill J. "Lehi's Tree and Alma's Seed." In *Heroes from the Book of Mormon*. Salt Lake City: Deseret Book, 1995.

Benson, Ezra Taft. *The Teachings of Ezra Taft Benson*. Salt Lake City: Bookcraft, 1988.

Brown, Hugh B. *Eternal Quest*. Edited by Charles Manley Brown. Salt Lake City: Bookcraft, 1956.

Children's Songbook. Salt Lake City: The Church of Jesus Christ of Latter-day Saints, 1989.

Evans, Richard L. Conference Report. October 1964, 134–37.

Hinckley, Gordon B. "The Empty Tomb Bore Testimony." *Ensign*, May 1988, 65–68.

———. *Teachings of Gordon B. Hinckley*. Salt Lake City: Deseret Book, 1997.

Hymns of The Church of Jesus Christ of Latter-day Saints. Salt Lake City: The Church of Jesus Christ of Latter-day Saints, 1985.

Kimball, Spencer W. *Faith Precedes the Miracle*. Salt Lake City: Deseret Book, 1972.

———. "The Foundations of Righteousness." *Ensign*, November 1977, 5–6.

———. "God Will Not Be Mocked." *Ensign*, November 1974, 4–9.

———. "Listen to the Prophets." *Ensign*, May 1978, 76–78.

———. "The True Way of Life and Salvation." *Ensign*, May 1978, 4–7.

Lee, Harold B. *Teachings of Harold B. Lee*. Edited by Clyde J. Williams. Salt Lake City: Bookcraft, 1996.

Lewis, C. S. *The Problem of Pain*. New York: Touchstone, 1996.

Maxwell, Neal A. "Content with the Things Allotted unto Us." *Ensign*, May 2000, 72–74.

———. *If Thou Endure It Well*. Salt Lake City: Bookcraft, 1996.

———."In Him All Things Hold Together." Address delivered 31 March 1991. In *Brigham Young University 1990–91 Devotional and Fireside Speeches*. Provo: Brigham Young University, 1991.

———. *The Neal A. Maxwell Quotebook*. Compiled by Cory H. Maxwell. Salt Lake City: Bookcraft, 1997.

———. *Notwithstanding My Weakness*. Salt Lake City: Deseret Book, 1981.

———. "Patience." In *Speeches of the Year, 1979*. Provo: Brigham Young University, 1980.

McConkie, Bruce R. *Doctrinal New Testament Commentary*. 3 vols. Salt Lake City: Bookcraft, 1965–73.

Oaks, Dallin H. "Good, Better, Best." *Ensign*, November 2007, 104–8.

Packer, Boyd K. *Mine Errand from the Lord*. Salt Lake City: Deseret Book, 2008.

Smith, Joseph. *History of The Church of Jesus Christ of Latter-day Saints*. Edited by B. H. Roberts. 7 vols. Salt Lake City: The Church of Jesus Christ of Latter-day Saints, 1932–51.

Smith, Joseph F. *Gospel Doctrine*. Salt Lake City: Deseret Book, 1939.

Twain, Mark. *The Innocents Abroad*. Vol. 2. New York: Harper & Sons, 1911.

Uchtdorf, Dieter F. "Happiness, Your Heritage." *Ensign*, November 2008, 117–20.

———. "We Are Doing a Great Work and Cannot Come Down." *Ensign*, May 2009, 75.

Voices from the Past: Diaries, Journals, and Autobiographies. Compiled by Campus Education Week Program. Provo: Brigham Young University, Division of Continuing Education, 1980.

Young, Brigham. *Discourses of Brigham Young*. Compiled by John A. Widtsoe. Salt Lake City: Deseret Book, 1977.

PHOTOGRAPHY CREDITS

Janey Top Kauffman: pages xiv, 6, 58

Brent L. Top: pages ii, xii, xvi, xviii, 3, 4, 5, 9, 10, 16, 19, 22, 23, 26, 35, 36, 38–39, 40, 45, 48, 52, 54, 56, 57, 59, 72, 77, 82, 84, 85, 86, 97, 98, 106, 110, 116, 121

N. Ferris Top: pages viii, xvii, 12, 15, 20, 31, 32, 34, 65, 78, 80, 109, 111, 112, 122

Jupiter Images Unlimited: pages 29, 46, 62, 74, 89, 90, 95, 96, 101, 102, 103, 105, 114, 117, 119, 120

Shutterstock: pages xi, 24, 60, 66, 68, 92, 94, 108, 115